Da Vinci's
KITCHEN

ALSO BY DAVE DEWITT

Precious Cargo:
How Foods From the Americans Changed the World

The Founding Foodies:
How Washington, Jefferson, and Franklin
Revolutionized American Cuisine

The Chile Pepper Encyclopedia

The Complete Chile Pepper Boook
(with Paul W. Bosland)

1,001 Best Hot & Spicy Recipes

The Southwest Table

A World of Curries

Growing Medical Marijuana

Callaloo, Calypso & Carnival:
The Cuisines of Trinidad & Tobago
(with Mary Jane Wilan)

Microfarming for Profit

New Mexico: The Land of Enchantment

The Hot Sauce Bible
(with Chuck Evans)

The Whole Chile Pepper Book
(with Nancy Gerlach)

Da Vinci's
K I T C H E N

A Secret History of
Italian Cuisine

DAVE DeWITT

**SUNBELT
EDITIONS**

ALBUQUERQUE, NEW MEXICO

SUNBELT EDITIONS

Sunbelt Editions
P.O. Box 4980
Albuquerque, NM 87196
www.SunbeltEditions.com

ISBN-13: 978-0-9832515-3-8
ISBN-10: 0-9832515-3-3

Proofreading by Rebecca Green & Yara Abuata
Cover design and art by Lois Manno
Additional interior illustrations by Lois Manno and Kelli Bergthold
Index by Michelle B. Graye

*To the memory of my mentor: the late, great Frank Crosby,
self-proclaimed "Mr. Terrific" and show producer extraordinaire.*

ACKNOWLEDGMENTS

Thanks to the following people for assisting in making this challenging project a reality:

Kelli Bergthold, Paul Bosland, Marco Budinis, Nancy Carter, Danise Coon, Mario Dadamo, Rick and Kim DeWitt, Gwyneth Doland, Nancy and Jeff Gerlach, Margaret Henderson, Lois Manno, Scott Mendel, Lisa Rogak, Wayne Scheiner, Mary Jane Wilan, Glenn Yeffeth, and Harald Zoschke.

Foreword

It was like, a literary agent and a client walked into a bar and started scribbling on napkins until they had an idea for a new book, but this one happened on the phone.

"Dave, could you write a book entitled *Da Vinci's Kitchen?*" That would be my long-time agent Scott Mendel on the phone.

"Except for the fact that I know next to nothing about Da Vinci or his kitchen, sure." There it was, scribbled on the digital napkin, *Da Vinci's Kitchen.*

It turned out that one of Scott's other clients, Lisa Rogak, the author of *The Man Behind the Da Vinci Code: An Unauthorized Biography of Dan Brown*, had suggested that there was a possible book about Da Vinci and his food. Scott took the ball and ran with it, right to me. So I cobbled together some ideas and wrote a proposal for *Da Vinci's Kitchen*, and sure enough, Glenn Yeffeth, owner of Ben Bella Books in Dallas, bought the U.S. hardcover rights. So I got to work, plowing my way through a lot of Da Vinci material. I did discover his shopping lists that were collected in his Notebooks, so I basically knew what staples he had in his larder. With some trepidation, I wrote a first draft.

My editor at Ben Bella promptly rejected it with a note that said, "Too much Da Vinci, not enough kitchen." A lot of authors would have been crushed, but I was elated because I felt that I was somewhat freed from having to force Da Vinci into every chapter. I could make the Da Vinci story just one chapter (the title chapter) and in the rest of them I could write about how introduced crops and foods completely changed Italian cuisine, like rice, sugar, durum wheat (hard wheat, for pasta), tomatoes, and chile peppers. The second draft was accepted and the book was published. It got very little recognition in the U.S. but eventually sold out the first edition. For some unex-plained reason, the publisher decided not to reprint and reverted the U.S. rights back to me.

But Scott was busy selling rights to foreign editions, explaining to me that Europeans and Asians were much more interested in Da Vinci than Americans. It took a few years, but Scott sold editions that were published in China, Czech Republic, Hungary, Japan, Korea, Lithuania, Poland, Russia, Slovakia, Taiwan, and Turkey. Since I didn't have to do any work at all on those editions, it was like finding a bag of money in the street each time one sold!

And now, I'm making *Da Vinci's Kitchen* available in ebook form at a very reasonable price.

CONTENTS

Preface

The Cast of Characters

Any history of food must also be about people, and this book is no exception. Because the most important characters in this book are not confined to their own chapters but make appearances throughout the narration, I'm giving brief introductions here.

Leonardo da Vinci
(1452–1519)

Leonardo's role here is primarily that of a catalyst, as he gave me the incentive to research and write this book. Reading several of his biographies triggered a "where's the food?" response in this food writer and prompted me to study his notebooks to find the food references in them. Amazingly, I even found his recipe for a salad dressing. The contents of Leonardo's larder, his philosophy of food and life, and his kitchen inventions provided a springboard for me to explore the foodways of Renaissance Italy. Leonardo is also involved in a controversy regarding the date of the introduction of corn, or maize, into Italy, which I discuss in chapter seven.

Many labels have been stuck on Leonardo. The most commonly used are painter, sculptor, draftsman, scientist, architect, engineer, anatomist, inventor, musician, mathematician, and the "ultimate Renaissance man." He lived during an extraordinary time, the beginning of the Renaissance, and his contemporaries, including some friends and acquaintances, were Niccolo Machiavelli, Sandro Botticelli, Rafael, Titian, Cesare Borgia, Benvenuto Cellini, the kings of France Louis XII and Francis I, Michelangelo, Giuliano de' Medici, Hieronymus Bosch, Copernicus, and Donatello, among others. One of Leonardo's most talented biographers,

Leonardo's vision of himself in later years
Sunbelt Archives

Charles Nicholl, commented about this period in time: "The old beliefs are crumbling; it is a time of rapid transition, of venal political strife, of economic boom and bust, of outlandish reports from hitherto unknown corners of the world. The experience of the Renaissance—not yet defined by that word, not yet accounted as a 'rebirth'—is one of disruption as much as optimism."

MAESTRO MARTINO
(DATES OF BIRTH AND DEATH UNKNOWN)

Martino, sometimes called "Martino of Como," was the author of *Libro de arte coquinaria* (*Book on the Art of Cookery*), which he wrote between 1460 and 1465. It is regarded as the first "modern" cookbook because of the quality of the recipes, but it was not a printed book, appearing only in handwritten form. Not much is known about Martino, but his influence on Italian cooking was very significant.

PLATINA
(BARTOLOMEO SACCHI, 1421–1481)

Platina took Martino's book, borrowed the recipes with credit, added his own comments on various foodstuffs, and published his own book, *De honesta voluptate et valetudine* (*On Right Pleasure and Good Health*). It was written between 1465 and 1468 and is generally regarded as the first printed cookbook, appearing in 1472 (some say 1475). Platina, famous in his own right because of this book, also helped spread the word of Martino's talent by using his recipes. Platina was also the first librarian of the Vatican.

BARTOLOMEO SCAPPI
(C. 1540–1570)

Scappi, not to be confused with Sacchi, was the chef of Pope Pius V. He wrote *Opera dell'arte del cucinare*, or *Work on the Art of Cooking*, which is usually just called Opera. It was published in Venice in 1570, the year of his death. The book went through many printings, profoundly influencing the chefs who followed him. He is well known for perfecting the design and use of the Renaissance kitchen.

LUDOVICO SFORZA
(1451–1508)

The duke of Milan, Sforza was Leonardo's benefactor and sponsor during those productive years in Milan. He was a patron of the arts who supported agriculture and sponsored elaborate feasts with spectacles that Leonardo produced.

CATHERINE DE' MEDICI
(1519–1589)

An Italian who married the king of France, Catherine is given credit (by the Italians) for greatly improving the food of the French court. This controversial story is told in chapter six.

SALAI
(GIACOMO CAPROTTI, 1480–1524)

Salai ("little devil") was Leonardo's longtime companion, servant—and some say, his love interest.

A NOTE ON THE RECIPES

Although this project was not designed to be a cookbook but rather a food history, I found it impossible to ignore the recipes that I came across in my research, because, after all, they are what best preserve the primary material in the history of cooking. I decided to treat recipes in two ways: either preserved in the words of the old masters (and edited), or as recipes in a modern style. There are many early recipes that are used as sidebars in the chapters' text—illustrating what was going on in the minds of these creative chefs who were creating the earliest cookbooks. For the recipes in a modern style, I chose to limit them to a maximum of five recipes per chapter, select them very carefully, and place them at the end of each chapter. There are a couple of reasons for this: first, I wanted to examine how early ingredients are still used and how the recipes made with them are prepared today. Secondly, I figured that since only experienced and adventurous cooks would attempt to recreate any of the early recipes, I would give us average cooks a way to experience the flavors of the two Italian "renaissances of cuisine" with a select group of easy-to-follow recipes that reflect the chapter they are placed in.

Some style notes:

Olive oil—use the best that you can afford or find.
Parmesan—a generic term referring to various hard cheeses; use Italian brands if possible.

Chapter One

Regional Cuisines
That Survived the Wars

We tend to think of the Renaissance as a glorious period of time devoted to the arts, culture, and science. But there was a dark side to the Renaissance that was christened by invasions, wars, and famine.

The City-States

"In Florence, Leonardo was at the heart of refined humanism," writes historian Alessandro Vezzosi, "a brilliant world of literary and artistic ferment and an extraordinary melting pot in which Tuscan tradition was enriched with a revival of interest in classicism and new influences from the north." During Leonardo's time, the population of Florence was about 150,000, and the city was on an equal footing with the major powers of Europe: France, England, the Holy Roman Empire, and Milan. There was no Italy or universal Italian language at this time; rather in what is now Italy, there were a number of city-states, including the Republic of Florence, the Duchy of Milan, the Venetian Republic, the Republic of Siena, the Republic of Genoa, and so on. Each city-state had its own dialect, but that was gradually changing since Dante Alighieri used both Tuscan and Sicilian in his *Divine Comedy* in the fourteenth century. Among the city-states, alliances shifted, borders changed, and diplomatic relations were volatile for hundreds of years. The good news was that trade and banking were flourishing; the bad news was the ongoing, destructive wars among the city-states.

Trade between the city-states of Italy and other Mediterranean and northern ports, which had severely declined during the Middle Ages, re-

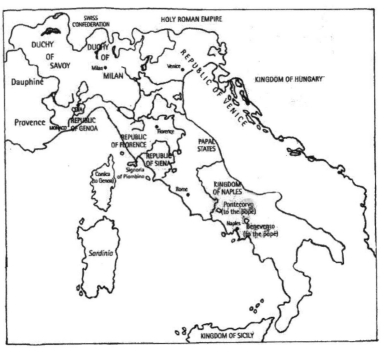

Map of the Italian city-states, c. 1490
Sunbelt Archives

bounded at the beginning of the Renaissance as luxury goods were shipped into Italian ports such as Pisa, Genoa, and Venice. This trade increased cash flow to the city-states, which in turn stimulated the banking industry. Florence became the region's central banking city, and the flourishing banks included those of the powerful de' Medici family, which had branch banks in other cities.

Two other important factors influenced the beginning of the Italian Renaissance. Because the Ming Dynasty in China had stopped all trading with foreigners, the money that would have gone to purchase luxury goods from China was instead invested in the Italian city-states, and the rich, ruling merchant class and a wealthier Church commissioned a great number of works of art and architecture, benefiting artists such as Leonardo.

The invention of the printing press and the publication of the Gutenberg Bible in 1452, the year of Leonardo's birth, was another innovation that improved the culture. Within a few decades, presses were established throughout the city-states that printed affordable copies of classical texts and other works. Not only were libraries repositories of knowledge, but perennial students like Leonardo could buy printed books rather than expensive, hand-copied volumes.

The beginning of the Italian Renaissance did lack one important factor: peace. The political nature of Italy was confusing and unstable. Fifteenth- and sixteenth-century Italy has been compared to a miniature continent where the city-states were in effect warring counties. It is ironic that the intellectual and artistic triumphs were happening in a world of violence and war. Milan warred against Venice, Florence against Pisa, Rome against Florence, Naples against Milan. Alliances were made only to fall apart, and the city-states were ravaged constantly by pillage, rapine, and battle. During the Italian Renaissance, the old bonds of the society of the Middle Ages were broken, and new ones were forged.

THE FIRST ITALIAN FOOD RENAISSANCE

One of the new bonds of society was the changing food habits of the region. The pre-Renaissance food of the Italian city-states, as well as southern France, much of Spain, and North Africa, was based on wheaten bread, olive oil, fish, eggs, a variety of vegetables, meat such as mutton and lamb, and an abundance of wine. The food historian Roy Strong comments about Renaissance changes: "Basically the old medieval core remained intact, but it was enlarged, refined, and enriched as the sixteenth century progressed. The same spices continued to be used, although reduced in range. Their presence, indicating expense, was central to the parade of wealth which was the essence of court cookery."

OF THE WINES OF ITALY

"Italy yields excellent wines, and the common red wine is held very nourishing, so as the fairest women will dine with the same and a sop of bread dipped into it, thinking it will make them fat (which kind of women the Venetians most love, all things being equal), yea, and more fair."

—Fynes Moryson, An *Itinerary*, 1617

Any discussion of the changing cuisine refers almost exclusively to the foods eaten by the wealthy, who could exercise freedom of choice in what they were eating. They could choose to eat bread and water, or they could choose cake and wine. The poor peasants, of course, had no such choice.

Beef, which during the Middle Ages was regarded as appropriate for the lower class but not for the wealthy table, now had greater status, with veal being the prized meat of the cow because it was slaughtered while quite young. The very fact that a nobleman could kill a calf was a sign of wealth and prestige. Conversely, other foods that we would find repugnant today were regarded as the epitome of dining: noses, eyes, cheeks, livers, bowels, heads, kidneys, tripe, tongues, sweetbreads, cockscombs, and testicles of animals, along with a similar list of fish parts. This explains the curious "Dish of Trout Intestines," which appears in two classic Italian cookbooks of the time.

Other influences on Italian Renaissance food came from the Middle East. During the Crusades, Europeans had discovered Saracen cuisine in Arab lands, including a number of ingredients that had been little known or unknown in Western Europe. Food historian C. Anne Wilson notes, "The introduction of Saracen-inspired dishes in the West began in noble and royal households," and the new ingredients included sugar, almonds, pistachios, rice, dates, citrus fruits, pomegranates, rose water, and spinach. One new technique that was introduced was thickening sauces and stews with ground almonds. Marzipan, an almond paste bound with sugar, was commonly served as a dessert at the end of a meal.

And classical writers influenced the way foods were prepared. The humoral theory, dating back to the ancient Greek physician Galen, dominated medieval medicine and was carried into the Renaissance through the link between food and medicine. Basically, the theory holds that all living things contain four elements, or humors: blood, choler, phlegm, and melancholy. These correlated with air, fire, water, and earth, respectively. In the kitchen, it was necessary for the cook to balance the four natures of these humors: hot, dry, wet, and cold. Food not prepared with the humors in mind would be unhealthy to eat, and certain foods were prepared in ways thought to balance the humors. For example, beef was boiled because it was considered to be "dry" and "cold," but pork was roasted to dry out its "wet" humor. Fish was considered "wet" and "cold," so it was fried to dry it out and warm it up.

"In general," writes food historian Jean-Louis Flandrin, "the 'coldest' and 'crudest' meats were the ones served with the hottest, spiciest sauces." Since poultry was the noblest meat in the food chain, it merely required *jance*, a mixture of white wine, cider vinegar, ginger, and cloves. The humoral theory applied to texture as well, and many dishes contained ground or minced ingredients, because the humors were thereby mingled together and thus more easily digested.

The humoral theory was advanced by the cookbook writers of the time, who borrowed from the past but were influenced by the trade in foodstuffs from other countries. These writers "shared a similar attitude toward food," notes food historian Ken Albala, "generally open, eclectic, and international."

THE BASIC FOODS OF THE PERIOD

Some writers on the food of the Renaissance have observed that the Italians had three staples: bread, wine, and everything else. In reality, that's a fairly accurate comment about the peasant class, but it hardly applies to the more varied diets of the courts of the city-states. Food historian Allen Grieco points out the little-known fact that the cost of wheat flour was surprisingly high when compared to the cost of meat. Today meat is roughly fifteen times the cost of flour, but in early Renaissance Italy, pork was only twice as expensive as wheat flour, and veal cost only two and a half times as much. But there was a direct social link here: "The lower a person's social rank, the greater percentage of income spent on bread."

This was also true for wine. In fact, in a study by Louis Stouff of the food budget of the Studium Papal (Pope's School) in Provence circa 1365, the following percentages were found:

Wine: 41%
Bread: 32%
Meat: 15.5%
Fish, eggs: 5.3%
Spices, cooking fat, cheese: 3.1%
Fruit, vegetables: 3%

Food writer Clifford A. Wright asks, "What do these figures tell us? Without question they tell us that in Provence, wine is food and the vaunted 'Mediterranean vegetables' barely existed." However, most vegetables were probably not purchased but rather grown in gardens.

Even if the higher classes spent less of their food budgets on bread, it was still baked in the royal courts as well as in peasant kitchens. Platina gives this advice on baking bread:

I recommend to anyone who is a baker that he use flour from wheat meal, well ground, and then passed through a fine sieve to sift it; then put in a bread pan with warm water; to which has been added salt, after the manner of the people of Ferrari in Italy. After adding the right amount of leaven, keep it in a damp place if you can and let it rise. That is the way bread can be made without much difficulty. Let the baker beware not to use more or less leaven than he should; in the former instance, the bread will take on a sour taste, and in the latter it becomes heavy and unhealthful and is not readily digested. The bread should be well baked in an oven, and not on the same day; bread from fresh flour is the most nourishing of all, and should be baked slowly.

THE PLEASURE OF WINE

"The only time I've ever seen you cheerful...was when we were tasting that red wine, do you remember? You forgot all about your worries....We laughed and talked all night...."

—Francesco Datini to Ser Lapo Mazzei, c. 1400

The social figures for bread and wine budgeting mentioned above were not true for *companagium*, the "everything else" that brought variety into the diet. Only 14 percent of a lowly shepherd's budget was spent on this item, while the overseers who ran the property spent up to 40 percent of their budgets on extras. "In short, bread occupied an increasingly conspicuous percentile share of the diets of the lower social classes," writes Grieco. "Inversely, this proportion shrank as one rose through the social hierarchy."

Wine, too, was seen as an aristocratic beverage, much more so than beer. Water was last on the list. One story goes that a traveler in the province of Emilia asked a peasant for a drink of water. "*Signor mio*," the good peasant replied, "water makes even the fence posts rot. But some wine I will give you willingly."

The Italian Renaissance was also the birth of wine as more than just a beverage to drink with bread. "Wines now begin to be carefully matched to courses," notes Roy Strong, "light white wines for the antipasti, red for the roasts, and on through fortified and intoxicating wines for dessert." Of course, the quality of the wine depended on what social class it was being served to. Peasants had to make do with the cheap stuff that was pressed out of the leftover grapes, which had already been crushed once for the quality wine for the upper class. "People chose their wine on the basis of their social standing," writes food historian Odile Redon, "their occupation, their age, and their constitution." Whites and clarets were more appropriate for the upper classes, who were regarded as more "refined" and "delicate." Red wines were considered to be more nourishing for manual laborers, and it is no coincidence that they were cheaper. Wine was often diluted with water to make it go further and to lower the alcoholic content of each glass.

USES OF THE GRAPE VINE

"The vine which without comparison is the greatest commoditie of Tuscany, if not Italy, hath these uses. Of the Grape they feed, of the juyce they make Wine; of the shreddings they make small bundles, like our Fagots; of their leaves feed their Oxen; & lastly of the stones they feed their Pigions."

—Sir Robert Dallington, 1605

Leonardo himself believed in diluted wine, writing in his notebooks, "Let your wine be mixed [with water], take little at a time, not between meals, and not on an empty stomach." Leonardo, it seems, was a moderate kind of guy and not much of a drinker.

THE ITALIAN SPICE TRADE

The historian Jean-Louis Flandrin observes: "At no time in European history did spices play as great a role as in the fourteenth, fifteenth, and sixteenth centuries, and at no time were they as important in cooking, to judge by their variety, frequency of use, and the quantities utilized." The Republic of Venice was the major city-state involved in the spice trade. Venice had provided the ships that carried the Crusaders to the Holy Land during the eleventh century, and those vessels returned with pepper and other spices bought in Alexandria. A single large Venetian ship returning from Alexandria could carry in her hold spices worth 200,000 ducats, and the estimated value of the Venetian spice trade was millions of ducats a year.

Spice caravans from Asia supplied Europe's demand for spices.
North Wind Picture Archives

So Venice became the major spice city, and pepper was the number one spice, with Europeans importing more than six and a half million pounds a year. Although pepper was only one of many spices traded, it accounted for well over half of all spice imports into Italy. And no other spice came within one-tenth the value of pepper. Why was it so beloved? Food historian Henry Hobson notes: "No spice except pepper made edible heavily salted meat, when no other form of preservation except salting was generally employed in Europe. Salt and pepper stood between carnivorous man and starvation, especially at sea, in the hungry months, and if crops failed."

PERFECT STRONG SAUCE

"If you want to make a strong sauce, take cloves and cinnamon and a little cardamom and hazelnuts that have been cooked on hot coals so that their skins can be rubbed off, and a little of the inside of the bread and sugar. Pound these together a little and add vinegar and this is a good sauce for all roasts."

—from *Libro per cuoco*, c. 1500

And the historian Wolfgang Schivelbusch adds: "Besides being used in food, spices were presented as gifts, like jewels, and collected like precious objects." He goes on to point out that several factors caused pepper and other spices to be linked to Paradise: their strong bite, their exotic origin, and their exorbitant cost. "Pepper, cinnamon, and nutmeg were status symbols for the ruling class, emblems of power which were displayed and then consumed. The more sharply pepper seared their guests' palates, the more respect they felt for their host." It is often thought that pepper and other hot spices were used to disguise spoiled meat, but this is unlikely. The use of hot spices in quantities which modern diners would judge to be intolerable was not, as popularly believed, the way that cooks disguised the bad smells and flavors of rotting meat. The accounts reveal that the rich households that used the most spices had adequate if not plentiful supplies of meat, game, and fish. Besides, the authorities were well aware of hygiene, and butchers were forbidden to sell tainted meat; meat and fish that were not sold within one day of catch or slaughtering were required to be salted. Several historians have commented that the meat consumed, instead of being rotten, was probably insufficiently aged.

RENAISSANCE CARNIVORES, PART I

"Even more than modern Americans, Renaissance Italians consumed quantities of meats that would induce protein shock in today's pasta-eating Italians. At a 'homey dinner' in Mantua in 1532, for example, eighteen gentlemen were served, besides salads, breads, fruits and sweets, eighteen plates of pheasant salads, five capons, 90 sausages, meatballs, liver dainties, five ducks, three tongues, five prosciutto and mortadella pastries, fifteen partridges, fifteen Milanese sausages, and a stag—during the first course."

—Berengario delle Cinqueterre

Cooks were buying all the spices they could get, according to recipes in early cookbooks of the time. Two untitled English cookery books, known as the Harleian Ms. 279 (c. 1430) and the Harleian Ms. 4016 (c. 1450), call for heavy spicing of 90 percent of the meat and fish dishes. The most common spices in those two books are ginger, black pepper, mace, cloves, cinnamon, and galangal. "The medieval ruling classes had a peculiar penchant for strongly seasoned dishes," notes Wolfgang Schivelbusch. "The higher the rank of a household, the greater its use of spices." The recipes of both Martino and Platina, who were part of the nobility, call for heavy spicing. This was definitely a form of conspicuous consumption, and their recipes make it clear that the spices were associated with wealth, status, and prestige. Yes, a lot of spicing went on, but it was not random. There was a plan, a hierarchy of spicing that paralleled the hierarchy of the foods being spiced.

Another reason for the heavy use of spices in late medieval and early Renaissance times was their alternate use as a medicine. Every spice used in the kitchen was originally imported as a medicine and only later on was used as a seasoning. Physicians from the thirteenth to the beginning of the seventeenth century recommended heavily using spices to make meat more digestible. During this time, digestion was seen as a form of cooking in the stomach with the "animal heat" of the body, and since spices were viewed as hot, they assisted in the digestive process. Pepper was judged to be of the fourth degree of hotness and dryness, while cloves, galangal, and cardamom were of the third degree; cinnamon, cumin, cubeb pepper, and nutmeg were of the second degree; and so on.

Interestingly, although spices were used to assist in digestion, they were banned if a person became ill. Anyone who suffered a fever could not use them because they were hot and dry and would only make the fever worse. Food for the sick was always boiled, and instead of using spices, most of the dishes were seasoned with sugar, the most "temperate" of condiments.

Of course, the basic reason for the use of spices in the cooking of any age is that it improves the flavor of the dishes and spices up bland food. But spices also tend to kill bacteria—and those two theories are inseparable. Jennifer Billing and Paul W. Sherman, authors of "Antimicrobial Functions of Spices: Why Some Like It Hot," note that recipes are a record of the never-ending competition between us and the parasites that are competing with us for the same food. And everything that we do with our food, including washing it, drying it, cooking it, salting it, or spicing it, is a way to keep from being poisoned by these parasites. And many of the spices used have antimicrobial properties. They conclude: "We believe the ultimate reason for using spices is to kill food-borne bacteria and fungi."

During the time of Leonardo, spices were at an all-time high of popularity, but that would not last. The problem with the Venetian spice trade was the torturous route that pepper and other spices took: they were moved from India to Egypt and Syria, then transported across the Isthmus of Suez to Alexandria, then loaded and shipped to Venice, and then

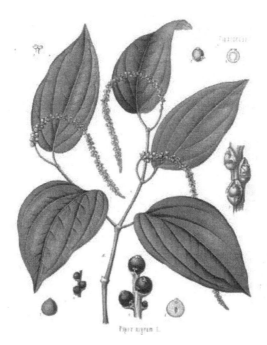

Black pepper was the most popular spice in Italy during Leonardo's time.
Sunbelt Archives

expensively transported over the Alps to central and northern Europe. When the prices the Venetians charged became too much, other nations entered the arena. Clearly, a sea route from India to Europe was necessary to eliminate the middlemen. After the sea route to India was discovered, the Portuguese and later the Dutch took over the spice trade from Venice. And when this happened, spice prices dropped radically, and more people could afford them. This rendered them less exotic and more ordinary. This fact, combined with middle- and late-Renaissance dietitians warning to use spices more sparingly, caused a decline in the use of spices in Europe.

The Renaissance cooks had a wide variety of spices to choose from, including three types of pepper: black pepper (*Piper nigrum*), long pepper (*Piper longum*), and cubeb pepper (*Piper cubeba*). Additionally, their cupboards might hold cinnamon, pepper, Grains of Paradise (Melegueta pepper), cumin, nutmeg, mace, saffron, and cloves. The spices were usually powdered and added to the liquid of the dish, or the sauce, which then was strained before being added back to the dish. This method, which ensured that the spices were not cooked with the food, allowed the spices to retain their most intense flavors.

The herbs and other flavorings used in the Renaissance kitchen were parsley, fennel, marjoram, mint, sage, rosemary, oregano, thyme, dill, basil, garlic, shallot, and onion. The latter three—even though they were thought to be the least "noble" of vegetables—still made an appearance in genteel dishes.

THE HIERARCHY OF ANIMAL FLESH

Educated people of Renaissance Italy believed that all things from the earth, water, air, and fire were organized according to the "Great Chain of Being." It was a concept of the world's structure that was accepted by most educated men from the time of Lucretius until the Copernican revolution and the Renaissance. The Great Chain of Being is composed of a great number of hierarchal links, from the most base and foundational elements (like rocks) up to the very highest perfection—in other words, God. Plants and animals were viewed according to how high they ranked on the chain. Bulbs such as onions ranked the lowest, and mythical animals such as the phoenix ranked the highest, as they were in the fire zone and just below God. Each plant or animal was thought inferior to the one above it and superior to the one below it, so no two plants or animals could have the same degree of nobility.

The lowest forms of animal life were the bottom-feeding shellfish like oysters and clams. Above them were the shrimp, crabs, and lobsters, and the fish came next on the chain. The highest water animals were whales and dolphins, which were hunted at the time. Because they swam at the surface of the ocean, they were thought to be striving for the air, and this gave them some degree of nobility.

BOLOGNA HISTORY

The most famous sausage of Bologna, Mortadella Bologna, dates back to the sixteenth century. It is now produced in the regions of Emilia-Romagna, Lombardy, Veneto, Tuscany, the Marches, Latium, and the province of Trento.

Placed in the Great Chain of Being between the dolphins and the birds were the land animals, with pigs at the bottom, mutton in the middle, and beef, particularly veal, at the top of this section of the chain. This left the birds in the air as the noblest food, and their order was ducks and geese (water birds) at the bottom, chickens in the middle, and songbirds at the top. Allen Grieco explains how this worked in a court feast:

> At banquets, such as the one that was held in honor of Nan-nina de' Medici to Bernardo Rucellai in 1466, veal was given to the people who came from the country properties of these two families, whereas the most important guests were served capons, chickens, and other fowl. In the hierarchy of meats, mutton (very much the everyday fare of the merchant classes) was placed below veal, and pork occupied the lowest rank. The latter was looked down upon, especially when salted, probably because it was also the meat that was most available for the lower classes.

RENAISSANCE CARNIVORES, PART 2

In January 1491, at the banquets for the wedding of Anna Sforza to Alfonso d'Este in Ferrara, 45,000 pounds of meat were consumed in one week. How was this paid for? Alfonso's father, Duke Ercole d'Este, took some extraordinary measures to raise revenues sufficient to conduct the wedding in a grand style, including the imposition of additional taxes and the forcible removal of art objects and decorations from the outlying area.

But none of this ranking hindered the development of cuisine and recipes; indeed, the works of both Martino and Platina delve into most of the ingredients available at the time, regardless of their relative nobility. The greatest number of recipes for meat in Martino's book are for veal, but he doesn't forget about the lesser meats:

To Make Sausages
If you want to make good sausages of pork or other meat, use meat that is both fat and lean, without sinews, and chop it very small. To ten pounds of meat, add one pound of salt, two ounces of nice clean fennel seeds, and two ounces of coarsely ground black pepper, mix everything together, and leave them for a day. Then take some very well-cleaned intestines, fill them with the mixture, and hang to dry in the smoke.

Note that despite the lower ranking of pork, it was judged to be good enough to use in sausages. Other meats, some judged to be dangerous by the physicians, were eaten by wealthy people because of snobbery or ostentation. "Dangerous" foods included fruit, venison, river fish, lamprey, and porpoise, but they were seasoned and cooked in ways that would supposedly render them safe. The lowest animal life commonly eaten were shellfish, provided that one lived within about sixty miles of the coast. The highest form of food that could be served was a peacock reclothed in its own plumage and breathing fire (see the recipe in chapter six from Martino).

Besides poultry and veal, other favored meats included the spring specialties of suckling pig (the highest form of pork), kid, and lamb. In the summer, the most commonly consumed meat was mutton. Sources vary about the use of game in Renaissance cooking, with one researcher claiming that it was uncommon, and another that it was widely used in rural areas but not in the royal courts. In my study of the recipes of Martino and Platina, I found mentions of boar, bear, and roe deer, but not many recipes for game, unless songbirds and rabbits are included.

But how were these meats being cooked? Here's what Martino advises:

> The gross flesh of the steer and cow must be boiled. The flesh
> of the calf is good boiled, and the loin roasted; the haunch is
> good in meatballs. All the flesh of the sheep is good boiled,
> except for the shoulder and leg, which are roasted. The flesh
> of the hog is unhealthy in any preparation. The flesh of the
> goat is good in January with garlic sauce. All of the hare is
> good roasted. The flesh of the bear is good in a pie.

During Lent and on Wednesdays and Fridays, meat was forbidden, and fish was the order of the day. Bream, shad, carp, trout, pike, eel, and sturgeon were the most commonly consumed freshwater fish (either fresh or salted), while sole, mackerel, tuna, cod, and red mullet were the saltwater fish most often eaten. Supplies of fresh fish were uncertain, and fish would spoil during the long trips inland, so most of the fish consumed away from the coasts were salted.

From Cabbage to Grapes

Medieval and Renaissance account books, which scholars use to track which foods were purchased and how much was spent on them by royal courts and monasteries, did not record vegetables because they were not part of the market economy. Like eggs and honey, they were produced at home and rarely showed up in the marketplaces where fish and meat were sold. Vegetables commonly grown in the most lowly peasant gardens to the more elaborate court gardens included cabbage, leeks, spinach, broad beans, lettuce, and parsnips. Other vegetables had a connection to Arab culture, like asparagus, artichokes, squash, melons, and eggplants. Of course, other vegetables, such as corn, potatoes, tomatoes, and chile peppers, were introduced into Italy after 1500, but it took them a long time to be accepted into Italian cooking. This story is told in chapter seven.

Fresh vegetables were eaten frequently in the summer and fall, but cabbage was king in the winter. Of course, cabbage keeps well, and there was plenty of it around during the winter. Cabbage boiled with salt pork was a very common peasant dish. Also used during the winter were the dried vegetables—peas, beans, chickpeas, and lentils. Often these were cooked in a beef broth to make a soup. Other winter foods included winter squash, which was dried and later reconstituted, and dried fruits such as raisins, figs, prunes, and nuts.

ON PEAS

"Peas are the noblest of vegetables, especially those whose pods are good to eat as well. They are cooked with herbs in both lean and fat dishes. For the latter, we simmer them in a good broth until half done, and then finish cooking them with a seasoning of hard bacon fat chopped with a knife or pounded in a mortar to the consistency of butter."

—Giacomo Castelvetro,
A Brief Account of the Fruit, Herbs and Vegetables of Italy, 1614

Despite the fact that proverbs going back to Roman times warned against eating salads ("A good salad is the beginning of an ill meal") because they were "cold," lettuce or spinach was often mixed with fresh herbs and "warmed up" with salt and olive oil. Interestingly, the cookbooks of the time have few salad recipes. Some food historians believe that Martino was silent on salads because it was so obvious that they were taken for granted by an accomplished cook like he was.

In the Great Chain of Being, despite being viewed by some as "dangerous," fruits were considered to be superior to all other plants and therefore acceptable for the upper classes to eat. The supposed nobility of fruit was due to the fact that most of it grew on bushes and trees, and thus grew higher off the ground than all produce such as onions. Grapes, figs, and the stone fruits like peaches have been a part of Mediterranean culture for millennia, but citrus fruits like oranges and lemons were introduced to southern Europe from India by the Arabs and were common in Italy from about the thirteenth century. Oranges were eaten as they are today, and lemon juice accompanied fried or grilled fish.

Grapes were not only used for wine, but in their unripe, sour form to make the sauce verjuice. They were also dried to make raisins. But a huge percentage of the grapes were used to make wine, and even Leonardo got into the wine business. In late August 1497, about the time Leonardo was finishing *The Last Supper*, Ludovico Sforza, at whose court Leonardo was living, deeded a plot of land to him. It was about three acres and included a vineyard, and Leonardo called it his "garden outside the walls of Milan." Not much is known about the vineyard, except that it measured 220 by 55 yards, and that Leonardo kept it until his death. Since we know he rented out one building on the property, he probably leased out the vineyard and shared the wine profits. The vineyard was still there as recently as the 1920s but is now a town garden.

Echoes of Vegetarianism

We have seen that root crops like onions and garlic were thought to be lowly, but they were still used in recipes eaten by both the court and the commoners. And when garlic was added in some form to a meat that was favored, such as poultry, it was "ennobled" and no longer thought of as inferior. Although the focus of the lavish banquets was on meat, Michel de Montaigne wrote in the sixteenth century in his *Travel Journal* of Italy, "This nation is not in the habit of eating much meat." While meat was predominant in England, France, and Germany, the Italian cooks elevated fruits, vegetables, and pasta to reach a status equal to that of meat. Because fish were eaten during fasting days, some varieties, particularly sturgeon, were regarded to be as good as meat. Scappi included twenty-three recipes for preparing sturgeon in his *Opera*, and his fasting day banquet depends almost entirely on that particular fish. Eels were also prized because they could be kept alive for days out of water, when transported in grass-lined baskets. "Fish is not inferior to the kinds of meat most often chosen to satisfy the palate," Scappi writes. "Indeed fish is the tastiest, most delicious food that Nature has provided."

Cheese was another meat substitute, and from the Middle Ages through the Renaissance, this "peasant food" gradually was ennobled, too, first during fasting days and eventually during Lent. Pantaleone da Confienza, the author of the oldest book on dairy products, *Summa lacticiniorum* (1477), wrote that cheese was consumed by "kings, dukes, counts, marquises, barons, soldiers, nobles, and merchants." Cheese was always a part of royal banquets; Messisbugo recommends "hard, fatty cheese" such as Pecorino, and Scappi loved "sliced Parmesan cheese" and mozzarella. Even their predecessor Platina noted in the middle of the fifteenth century that there were two cheeses "vying for first place" in Italy: marzolino from Tuscany and Parmesan from Parma. Interestingly, milk was not a wholly consumed beverage but was only a cooking or cheese-making ingredient; Platina believed that "[g]oat's milk is considered excellent…ewe's milk is next, with cow's milk in third place." The reason for this is probably the fact that milk spoiled so quickly because there was no refrigeration.

THE ROMAN CHEESE

Pecorino Romano is one of the oldest cheeses in existence, originating in Roman times in Latium. It was part of the daily rations of Roman legionnaires. These days, more than 67 million pounds of the cheese are produced each year, mostly in Sardinia.

The Italians made more use of vegetables than the other Europeans and were criticized for it. Costanzo Felici, who in 1569 wrote a treatise on gastronomic botany entitled *De' insalata e piante che in qualunque modo vengono per cibo del'homo* (*On Salads and Plants That in Some Way Become the Food of Men*), noted that "[s]alad foods, according to those who live beyond the Alps, are almost exclusive to greedy Italians, who have appropriated the food of those base animals that eat raw greens." Nevertheless, from Martino on, the great cookbook authors had recipes featuring such vegetables and herbs as cabbage, fennel, squash, lettuce, broad beans, peas, marjoram, mint, and parsley in soups, pies, and fritters.

Giacomo Castelvetro, an Italian exile living in England because he was Protestant, wrote a book in 1614 about "roots, greens, and fruits that are eaten in Italy" that was not published until after his death. "Italians eat more greens and fruit than meat," he proclaimed, and offered reasons why:

Franciscan monks in their vegetable garden, c. 1450
North Wind Picture Archives

The main reason is that our lovely Italy is not as attached to
meats as is France or this island [England]. For we must make
great efforts to find new foods to nourish the large number
of people found in such a small area of the earth. The other
motive, no less compelling than the one already given, is the
great heat experienced there nine months out of the year,
which makes us grow tired of meat.

The most popular vegetable of the late Renaissance was the artichoke.
Not mentioned in Martino's or Platina's works, it makes appearances in
Messisbugo's and Scappi's books, and Costanzo Felici, in the treatise mentioned above, notes: "They are the fruit of prickly or grasses that are known
by now to everyone. The craze for them has grown so much that they have
become familiar to all, and they enjoy an excellent reputation among the
great." These great people ate the artichokes both raw and cooked "on the
grill, on the fire, or in rich broth." Paolo Zacchia, in his 1636 book *Food*

for Lent, wrote, "It goes down smoothly when boiled; when roasted, it is easier on the stomach, and when truffled (as cooks describe it when it is flavored with wild mint, a small quantity of finely chopped garlic, pepper, oil, and salt), it reawakens the appetite."

There are a large number of purely vegetarian recipes in both Martino's and Platina's cookbooks, which was a fairly remarkable development. In the Middle Ages, it was the poor who ate vegetables, mostly in soups. But in the Renaissance, vegetables were being promoted for their health benefits—supposedly, they allowed diners to keep their minds free by not overburdening their stomachs. By overturning the old medieval preconception that meat was for the rich and vegetables were for the poor, the Italian cookbook authors were breaking new ground.

By far, the most important single vegetarian food of Renaissance Italy was pasta. Some form of it was known from Roman times—*lagana*, now known as lasagne. During the Middle Ages, cooks experimented with different shapes and cooking methods that continued into Renaissance times. The Romans baked their pasta, but Renaissance cooks boiled the fresh dough in water, milk, or a meat broth. They also used dried pasta, which could be easily stored, and drying transformed pasta from a handmade food to a commercial product. The major centers for commercial pasta production were Sicily, Liguria, and Genoa, and many of the early cookbooks referred to pasta as "Genoese." See chapter three for a more detailed discussion of macaroni, the generic term for dried pasta.

Martino was the first cook to give instructions on making vermicelli, or "little worms":

> Knead the pasta as above and make thin strips, that you shape
> into worm-like pieces with your fingers and allow to dry in the
> sun. They will keep for two or three years. When you begin
> to prepare them, cook in meat or good, rich chicken broth
> for an hour and serve up with grated cheese and spices. If not
> a meat day, cook them in almond milk and sugar, or goat's
> milk, but since milk does not need to be cooked as long as
> the vermicelli, boil them first in water as one does with rice.
> The same goes for *lasagne*, *tria*, and *formentini*. All these pasta
> dishes should be yellow with saffron, except for those cooked
> in milk.

Note the long cooking time for the pasta, for it seems that Renaissance cooks did not have the concept of *al dente* in their kitchens. It wasn't until the beginning of the seventeenth century that cooks suggested pouring cold water over cooked pasta to stop the cooking in order to make it firmer. The use of pasta in the kitchen was far different than it is today, and Scappi suggests "boiling domestic ducks, covered with macaroni, Roman-style," and "fat geese, boiled and stuffed, covered with *annolini*." These were, of course, banquet dishes in which pasta was served as a side dish, or just a part of the main course. For peasants, pasta—served with butter, cheese, sugar, and cinnamon, or maybe a spiced sauce—would be the main dish, and a vegetarian one at that.

SCAPPI'S LOMBARD-STYLE RICE

Take the shelled rice and cook it in broth that has been prepared by cooking capon, goose, and cervellate [pork sausage] and cooked until they are done. Take some of the rice and place it in a terracotta or silver or tin plate and sprinkle it with cheese, sugar, and cinnamon. Place some pieces of fresh 'butiro' cheese and pieces of the capon breast and goose with the cervellate cut in large pieces on the rice, and sprinkle it again with cheese, sugar, and cinnamon to make three layers. The top layer should be wet with freshly melted "butiro" cheese.

THE RENAISSANCE LARDER

Salt was a relatively expensive necessity in the Renaissance kitchen, and two types were used: a fine salt for the table and a coarser variety for cooking or the salting of meat and fish. Most of the Italian salt was imported from the mines of Ibiza, which also supplied northern Europe. Platina wrote about the importance of salt: "There must be salt on the table, lest the food seem bland, for we call a man foolish who is tasteless and insipid, because he has no salt in his character." It is interesting to note that salt is rarely mentioned in the recipes of Martino and Platina; apparently they left salt to be added at the table, although it was probably added to the broth used to boil pasta.

Speaking of pasta, food historian Clifford Wright notes: "The evidence is clear that by the fourteenth century, macaroni was well known.... Much of the early history of macaroni focuses on Sicily. We don't know if that is where it was invented, but we do know that it was a food eaten by the privileged aristocracy and by the Jewish population." Apparently pasta spread from Sicily up the peninsula. Another food historian, Odile Redon, adds: "We are obliged to shatter a beloved myth by noting that Marco Polo had nothing to do with this popularity; we find references to *maccaroni* (*maccheroni* in modern Italian) in texts dating from before his lifetime." There was a guild for pasta makers—the *Lasagnari*—in medieval Florence. A fuller discussion of pasta follows in chapter three.

In terms of dairy products, milk was highly perishable, and if sold by milk vendors in the city, it was sometimes watered down. Generally speaking, milk came more from goats and sheep than cows, especially in the more southerly parts of the peninsula. Butter was more common in the north of Italy than in the south, where olive oil was used in cooking. There is no mention of cream in the medieval and Renaissance cookbooks, which is something of a mystery. Eggs were commonly used, and sometimes in very basic ways. One recipe calls for them to be broken right into the embers of a fire!

There were two main types of cheese: a soft cheese like ricotta that was mainly made in the spring and was used to stuff fritters, and the hard cheeses for grating over vegetables and pasta that were usually made from sheep's milk. Cheeses were often made into pies, like in Martino's recipe for *torta di formaggio*, where "all the different cheeses that you think will taste good together" are melted together, mixed with whipped egg whites and the yolks, and poured into a crust and baked.

GRATONATA OF CHICKEN

"Cut up your chickens, fry them with pork fat and with onions, and while they are frying add a little water so that they cook up nicely in the pan; and stir them often with a large spoon; add spices, saffron, and sour grape juice and boil; and for each chicken take four egg yolks, mix them with sour grape juice and boil this separately; and beat everything together in the pan, and boil everything together with the pieces of chicken; and when it boils remove it from the fire and eat it."

—from *Libro della cucina del secolo XIV*

Also present in the larder was, naturally, pork fat in all of its forms: fresh and salted pork belly (bacon), fatback, and lard. It was extensively used for frying, making pie crusts, and to "lard" lean cuts of meat by inserting the fat into cuts in the roast.

Of course, no Renaissance larder would be complete without olive oil. Not only was it ubiquitous in cooking, it was used as a fuel for lamps, as an ointment, and as a lubricant. Leonardo, who was surrounded by olive groves most of his life, drew sketches of olive presses in his notebooks and was trying to design better presses to make some of the oils used in his painting. He even wrote one of his "prophecies" about olives: "There will pour down from the direction of the sky that which gives us food and light." The answer to this prophecy is "olives falling from olive trees." Despite the fact that many people had olive trees near their houses, there was trade in olive oil and merchants who specialized in it.

We have heard briefly from Martino and Platina in this chapter, and now we will take a detailed look at the cooks and their revolutionary cookbooks.

Spice and Sugar Mix

Bartolomeo Scappi, the cook to Pope Pius V, recommends this blend of sugar and spices for enhancing foods in his *Opera dell'arte del cucinare*, one of the most influential Italian Renaissance cookbooks. It still works today when sprinkled over meats or poultry.

INGREDIENTS

24 cinnamon sticks
1 ounce cloves
½ ounce sugar
½ ounce dried ginger
½ ounce grated nutmeg
¼ ounce Melegueta pepper (Grains of Paradise)
¼ ounce saffron

Break the cinnamon sticks into pieces, combine them with the rest of the ingredients in a spice mill, and grind to a fine powder. Store the mixture in an airtight jar; it will keep for 3 to 4 months.

YIELD: ½ cup

Fettuccine di Carciofi
(Baby Artichokes, Parma Ham, and Fettuccine)

That faddish vegetable of the early Renaissance is revived in this pasta dish
with a Renaissance of its own—baby artichokes, available year-round from
specialty food retailers. To prepare the baby artichokes, slice off the tops and
bottoms and remove any of the purple or pink leaves. Steam or boil them until
tender, then cut them into quarters, lengthwise.

INGREDIENTS

3 tablespoons butter
1 cup Parma ham, julienned
2 tablespoons shallot, chopped
1 teaspoon garlic, minced
1 cup chicken stock
4 cups hot cooked fettuccine
1½ cups cooked baby artichokes
¼ cup grated Parmesan cheese, or to taste
¼ cup black olives, chopped
Italian parsley, minced, for garnish

Melt the butter in a large skillet and sauté the ham, shallot, and garlic for
about 3 minutes. Add the chicken stock and bring to a boil. Add the fettuccini
and toss. Add the artichokes, stir, and heat through. Sprinkle with the Parmesan cheese and olives, garnish with the parsley, and serve.

YIELD: 4 servings

Pollo alla Cacciatore
(Hunter's Chicken)

"Alla cacciatore" translates as "hunter-style" and usually means a stewed dish of meat or poultry. Today, many ingredients are added to this dish, including carrots, celery, onions, and tomatoes. But this simple recipe from Umbria preserves the early days and the ingredients used then. Serve this dish with rice or a simple pasta.

INGREDIENTS

½ cup red wine vinegar
1 teaspoon fresh rosemary, chopped
2½ pounds chicken, cut up
½ lemon
¼ cup olive oil
Salt and freshly ground black pepper, to taste

In a bowl, combine the vinegar, rosemary, and salt and pepper and set aside. Rub the chicken pieces all over with the lemon, season with salt and pepper, and allow to sit for 10 minutes.

Heat the olive oil in a large skillet and slowly fry the chicken pieces for about 30 minutes, turning often, until they are golden brown.

Pour the vinegar solution over the chicken and boil rapidly, stirring constantly to loosen the residue at the bottom of the pan. Reduce the liquid to half and serve the chicken.

YIELD: 4 to 6 servings

Asparagi alla Parmigiana
(Asparagus with Cheese)

In Italy, asparagus is tied into bundles and cooked upright in a tall, narrow pan so that the bottoms boil or simmer and the tops are steamed. This is a classic recipe for the preparation of this popular spring vegetable, but feel free to add spices or substitute another cheese, such as Fontina.

INGREDIENTS

2 pounds asparagus, trimmed to fit inside a saucepan and tied into
  4 bundles
½ cup freshly grated Pecorino Romano cheese
⅓ cup butter
Salt and freshly ground pepper, to taste

Preheat the oven to 350° F.

Place the bundles in a saucepan filled with cold water to ⅓ of the way up the bundles. Cover and bring to a boil, then reduce the heat to a simmer and cook the asparagus, covered, until *al dente*, about 5 to 7 minutes, depending upon the thickness of the spears.

Remove the bundles from the water, unstring them, and place them on an oval baking dish. Sprinkle a little cheese over them and keep them warm in the oven.

Melt the butter in a small pan and pour it over the asparagus. Add the remaining cheese and salt and pepper to taste and place under the broiler for a short period of time, until the cheese forms a light brown crust.

YIELD: 6 to 8 servings

Chapter Two

THE FIRST SUPERSTAR CHEFS

 One part of the glory of the Renaissance was the rediscovery of the world of the classics of Greece and Rome, mostly by book publishing, and the attempts to recreate that world. There was one culinary classic that was rediscovered during Leonardo's time, Apicius's *De re coquinaria*, or *On the Art of Cookery*. Apicius was, of course, the late fourth-century A.D. Roman writer on food and cooking. Previously only available in manuscript form to scholars, *De re coquinaria* had an enormous impact when published as a book in 1498. "Suddenly there was revealed a very different cuisine," writes food historian Roy Strong, "that of a highly sophisticated society which cultivated the pleasures of the table and surrendered willingly to the temptations of the appetite without any feelings of guilt." Strong calls the impact of Apicius the "humanist revival of the foods of Antiquity," and this impacted Renaissance cuisine by reviving

---

FRESH FAVA BEANS IN MEAT BROTH

The following recipe is from Maestro Martino, and a nearly identical recipe appears in Platina, but with fava translated as "broad bean."

Take the beans and remove their skins by soaking them in hot water as you would with almonds, then cook them in good broth, with some nice salt meat as well. When you think they are done, put in some chopped parsley and mint. This dish needs to be somewhat green to make it look attractive. You can cook peas and other fresh legumes in the same way, but there is no need to soak them in hot water like fava beans. Just leave them as they are in their thin pods.

---

interest in truffles and other fungi, seafood and caviar, chopped meats and sausages, and vegetables like asparagus and cabbages that were now "endowed with the aura of Antiquity" and thus became fashionable. And, of course, with the rediscovery of classic works like that of Apicius, there was a revival of another sort—the gastronome who was devoted to the joys of cooking and eating. There would be a few more gastronomes during the Renaissance who led the way for the multitudes that we have today.

MARTINO AND PLATINA

Maestro Martino, author of *Libro de arte coquinaria*, which he wrote in about 1460, was a scholar and a cook who worked in the kitchen of the Sforza court in Milan but preceded Leonardo's arrival there. He also worked as the private cook for Pope Paul II and his successor, Sixtus IV. Roy Strong called his work "a book that signaled a new era in the history of cooking…a landmark on account of the clarity, organization, and exactitude with which the recipes are for the first time presented."

The "book" is really a handwritten manuscript bound with board and calf leather that measures nine-by-five-and-three-quarters inches. There are eighty-five leaves containing 240 recipes written in Italian rather than Latin. About one-quarter of the recipes are known to be from earlier manuscripts, and the rest are Martino originals.

TO PREPARE A SUCKLING PIG

This recipe from Maestro Martino reads remarkably like the method used by many barbecuers in the United States today—except for the part about turning the piglet inside out!

First make sure that it is well cleaned. Then cut it open the length of the spine, remove all the innards, and wash it really well. Then take the liver and chop it fine, along with some good herbs, some garlic chopped fine, a little good bacon, some grated cheese, a few eggs, some crushed peppercorns, and a little saffron. Mix all these things together and put them inside your piglet, first turning it inside out as one does with tench [carp] so that the skin side is inside, then sew it together and truss it well. Put it to cook on a spit or on a grill, but let it cook slowly so that it is well done, both the meat and the stuffing. Make a little basting sauce with vinegar, pepper, and saffron and take two or three sprigs of bay leaves, sage, or rosemary and keep sprinkling this all over the piglet. You can do the same with geese, ducks, cranes, capons, or chickens.

Cooks in an early Italian kitchen, stylized
North Wind Picture Archives

Martino scraps the classical method of opening a cookbook with fruit and sweeter things, but rather jumps right into the meat dishes in the first chapter. And his seasonings suggest what Renaissance Italian food was all about. "What is striking," writes Roy Strong, "is the sign of a move away from imported spices in favor of using native aromatic herbs such as mint, marjoram, parsley, garlic, fennel, bay, sage, and rosemary, although spices were still to reign until the middle of the seventeenth century."

Medieval cuisine historian Bruno Laurioux reflects on Martino's enormous achievement: "It is no wonder then that compared with works of the previous century, Martino's *Libro de arte coquinaria* was seen as avant-garde gastronomy.... The profoundly innovative character of Martino's work gave it a virtual monopoly of the Italian culinary scene for almost a century."

Prior to Martino, detailed specifications were not a feature of cookbooks, since they were written to persuade a large number of readers about the techniques or superiority of a given cooking style. In fact, just the opposite was true: food writers wrote primarily for themselves, and their notes were intended merely to remind them how to produce a desired effect given a list of ingredients. And good cooks, when presented with recipes that were not their own, would know the proper proportions and procedures to create the dish.

But there is perhaps another explanation for the scantiness of information contained in culinary manuals prior to Martino: the desire not to divulge professional secrets. Like chemists, doctors, dowsers, soothsayers, wood carvers, painters, silk dyers, and so on, cooks were quick to realize that their prestige (and compensation) would increase in proportion to their command of more knowledge—if, that is, it did not become an easily accessible commodity. Unlike the purported individualism of today's consumer capitalism, which boils down to the persistent push to keep up with the Joneses, Renaissance individualism was largely the outcome of a search for distinction. This did not mean acquiring what everyone else was induced to own, but possessing what no one had yet discovered. Even books, one of the earliest artifacts to be reproduced mechanically, were at times printed in such a way as to seem unique—with different bindings for the same edition, for example.

MARTINO'S MARZIPAN TART

Carefully shell and skin the almonds and pound them as fine as possible since they are not going to be sieved. Note that to make the almonds whiter, tastier, and sweeter in the mouth, they should be soaked in cold water for a day and a night or even more; in this way the skins can be removed just by rubbing them in your hands. Sprinkle with a little rose water when pounding them so that they don't become oily. To make this tart really sweet, use equal amounts of sugar and almonds, a pound or so of each if you like. Mix well with one or two ounces of rose water. Take some wafers made with sugar, soak them in rose water and line your tart dish with them, then put the mixture in, spread it out flat, sprinkle with more rose water and some powdered sugar, and press it down well with a spoon. Cook very slowly in the oven or on the hearth, like the other tarts, taking care to moderate the heat and checking frequently to make sure it does not burn. Remember that this tart needs to be on the whole somewhat low and thin, rather than too deep and thick.

But Martino's book would never have had the impact it did had it not been for the "plagiarizing" of it by the librarian of the Vatican, Bartolomeo Sacchi, known as Platina. His book, *De honesta voluptate et valetudine* (*On Right Pleasure and Good Health*), which was written between 1465 and 1468, is generally regarded as the first printed cookbook. It was first printed in 1472 (some say 1475). Of the 250 recipes in the book, 240 were taken directly from Martino's work. However, there are many original parts of Platina's book, including descriptions of herbs. It should be pointed out that the two men knew each other and may have collaborated for a time. Platina acknowledged Martino in his book: "Martino de' Rossi of Milan, prince of cooks in our time, from whom I learnt about cooking." There was no real concept of plagiarizing in those times—writers and artists commonly borrowed from each other without attribution, both in literature and fine art.

The word "voluptate," or pleasure, in the title derives from "voluptas," which in medieval Latin meant sin. Platina is promoting the idea that the physical pleasure of dining could be, in the proper circumstances, "honesta," or right. In this way, Platina legitimizes eating and drinking beyond mere physical necessity to emphasize the physical and emotional pleasures they can bring. So the book is modern and secular because there is no allusion to the Christian tradition, and it is practical because it covers such subjects as clean tableware. Platina brought the cookbook into the world of letters with his book, making food and dining acceptable subjects for discussions among the educated elite. The book also includes quotations from Cato, Virgil, and Apicius, so it was a revival of the classic Roman kitchen in addition to being so modern. And the fact that Leonardo had a copy of Platina's treatise in his personal library connects Leonardo to the early Renaissance culinary scene, as we shall see later.

PLATINA'S RED CHICKPEA SOUP

Wash a pound or more of chickpeas in warm water. When they are washed and put in a pot without water, where they will simmer, mix in, with your hands, half an ounce of groats, a little oil and salt, up to twenty crushed peppercorns, and a little ground cinnamon. Then put on the hearth and add nearly a gallon of water, with sage and rosemary added, and parsley roots chopped fine. Let it boil until it is reduced to eight cups. When it has been almost cooked, drop in a bit of oil.

Platina was a philosopher, historian, and humanist born in 1421 of obscure origins who later became the prefect of the Vatican Library—but not before he was imprisoned and tortured by Pope Paul II. Platina was protesting the dissolution by Paul II of the humanist organization in Rome, the College of Abbreviators, to which Platina belonged. He wrote a letter to the pope in protest, and the furious pontiff ordered him imprisoned in Castel Sant'Angelo under the threat of death in September 1464. He was held until January 1465, when Cardinal Gonzaga arranged his release, but that was not the end of his troubles with Paul II.

In 1468, the pope arrested numerous members of the Roman Academy. "From what is known of this informal group of friends," writes Mary Ella Milham, a translator of Platina's work, "they were intellectuals drawn from many levels of Roman life.... They shared a passion for ancient Rome, gave themselves classical nicknames within the academy and were suspected of conducting pagan rites and even worshipping pagan gods." These "paganists" were accused of a plot against the pope's life, confined to prison, and some were tortured. "Platina's right arm was so seriously damaged by torture that he needed rest and therapy upon his release," writes Milham, who goes on to say that Platina was innocent of the charges. "There was no proof that the academy, despite its occasional bizarre behavior, was generally anti-Christian," she notes.

PLATINA'S BROAD BEANS IN THE FRYING PAN

In a frying pan well greased with oil, fry broad beans which have been cooked and softened with onions, figs, sage, and several other herbs of choice, and put on a plank or disc spread in the form of a cake, and cover with spices.

Platina was released in early 1469, Pope Paul II died in 1471 and was replaced by Sixtus IV, who promptly made Platina a favorite, and Platina returned the favor by writing *The Lives of the Popes*. In 1475, Sixtus (who commissioned the building and decoration of the Sistine Chapel) appointed Platina to be the first librarian of the Vatican Library, which had several thousand volumes.

Historians are uncertain about the exact time frame of *De honesta voluptate et valetudine*, but agree that it predated the prison experiences, and the publication date is usually given as 1465. Platina and Cardinal Gonzaga spent the early summer of 1463 as guests of Cardinal Ludovico Trevisan in Albano. Trevisan's celebrated chef of the time was Maestro Martino. It is thought that Martino gave Platina a copy of his manuscript of *Libro de arte coquinaria*, and that became the source for about 40 percent of *De honesta voluptate et valetudine*, which contains 95 percent of Martino's cookbook. Platina writes: "[The cook] should be completely like the man from New Como [Martino], the chief cook of our age, from whom I have learned the art of preparing food."

Platina commented in an undated (and most revealing) letter to Cardinal Giacomo Ammannati-Piccolomini:

> Before my [first] prison term I wrote this little book, *On Right Pleasure and Good Health*, which I commend to your generosity, striving eagerly to win a patron for it. As you are aware, it deals with the business of all the food merchants, and creeps through the taverns, and is, therefore a greasy and sordid subject. But he who is versed in cookery is not far removed from genius, since the meals that are to be concocted are largely a matter of ingenious composition, and, therefore, he must be proficient in it; he who takes upon himself this work as a profession must inform himself. Of course in the last analysis, it appears to me a dry and unpolished subject, and therefore, I am cleaning it of imperfections which, I have recognized, must be eliminated without fail. Surely, because good judgment in these matters will mostly benefit the superiors, I place this book, however dreadful (it certainly takes a chance with inspiring the ingenious ones, if you like) in your hands for your kind consideration and criticism, hesitatingly and also conditionally.

He was criticized by the poet Jacopo Sannazaro:

> On the character, customs, life and death of the popes;
> You used to write. A sharp history lesson it was.
> Now, Platina, you write tractates on cooking millet
> For the popes themselves to eat.

Platina defends himself in a dedicatory letter to Cardinal Bartolomeo Roverella in Rome and archbishop of Ravenna (1445–1476), whose powerful patronage helped Platina to make *On Right Pleasure and Good Health* the first book on gastronomy ever printed.

[Some] upbraid me about food as if I were a gluttonous and greedy man and as if I were proffering instruments of lust and, as it were, spurs to intemperate and wicked people. Would that they, like [me], would use moderation and frugality either by nature or instruction; we would not see today so many so-called cooks in the city, so many gluttons, so many dandies, so many parasites, so many most diligent cultivators of hidden lusts and recruiting officers for gluttony and greed. I have written about food in imitation of that excellent man, Cato, of Varro, the most learned of all, of Columella, of C. Matius, and of Caelius Apicius. I would not encourage my readers to extravagance, those whom I have always in my writing deterred from vice. I have written to help any citizen seeking health, moderation, and elegance of food rather than debauchery, and have also shown to posterity that in this age of ours men had the talents at least to imitate, if not to equal, our ancestors in any kind of [writing].

PLATINA'S SICILIAN MACARONI

Beat well-sifted white flour with egg whites and rose water and plain water. When it is mixed, draw out into thin strips of dough in the manner of straw half a foot long. Hollow them out with a very thin iron rod—when you pull out the iron, you will leave them hollow. When dried in the sun, pasta of this sort will last two to three years, especially if it was under the waning moon of August. If it is cooked in rich broth and poured into serving dishes, it should be sprinkled with fresh butter and sweet spices.

Judging from the frenzy of reprints that immediately followed the first edition, there is little doubt that Platina's was the right book at the right time. It was reprinted in Venice in 1475, 1498, 1503, and 1517; in Louvain and Cividale del Friuli in 1480; in Bologna in 1499; in Strasbourg in 1517; in Cologne in 1529 and 1537; in Paris in 1530; and in Lyon and in Basel, 1541. By that date there had been sixteen Latin editions of Platina's book printed.

And of course, Platina, just like his fellow humanists, wrote in Latin. But a large number of readers trained in kitchen arts needed some help in translating his text, so the book's life was extended in an even greater number of translations: into Italian in 1487, 1494, 1508, and 1516; into German in 1530, 1533, 1536, and 1542; and into French in Lyon in 1505, 1528, 1548, and 1571, and in Paris in 1509, 1539, 1559, and 1567.

"The rapid distribution of *De honesta voluptate* can been seen as part of the spreading enlightenment of the Renaissance," writes cookbook expert Barbara Feret, "which increasingly recognized individual competence and inventiveness.... The work was very well received and evidently was a major factor in the development of cookery in Europe."

PLATINA AND LEONARDO

Leonardo had but one cookbook in his library, Platina's *De honesta voluptate et valetudine*. Even more influential than Martino, whose book was never printed, Platina, "the humanist trained in Greek philosophy," as Milham notes, "is now raising the consumption of food and drink to the philosophic level without reference to conventional Christian views.... As is only now becoming recognized, he was the first writer on food to expound some of the principles of modern gastronomy." She adds:

> Platina was sincere in his love of the fine and sophisticated
> table. He no doubt relished the simple garlic and onions he
> enjoyed with Pomponio, but he wrote too elegantly about the
> necessary ambiance of for pleasurable dining, which befitted
> a wealthy home, and heaped too much praise on Martino,
> one-time chef for the Sforzas at Milan and now in charge of
> Trevisan's famed table in Rome, to be unsympathetic to gas-
> tronomic ideals that could be attained only with wealth.... *De
> honesta voluptate*, then, is a complex amalgam of sources, influ-
> ences, and originality which cannot in any fairness be dubbed
> a "mere cookbook"... but like its author, is never dull, and its
> scope is wide as it takes its readers from an academy gathering
> on the Esquiline to fishing on the river Adda and to the exotic
> Middle Eastern habitats of peppercorns and cannabis.

Platina essentially took Martino's *Libro de arte coquinaria*, appropriated the recipes, used many other sources, especially Pliny the Elder, added his own observations, and created a book that is a very interesting read, even if today we would consider it to be a partial plagiarism. The books are so closely related that they share the same publication date of 1465; however, we must remember that there were different "editions" of Martino's handwritten volume and Platina's printed book.

"Platina's *De honesta voluptate et valetudine* became the first best-selling cookery book in history," notes Renaissance expert Gillian Riley. "His

An early Renaissance kitchen, c. 1518
North Wind Picture Archives

claim that his generation were better than the ancient authors they revered in at least one thing—cooking—gives an endearing insight into the cheerful enthusiasms of those early Roman Humanists. . . . It is interesting to compare Martino's recipes with Platina's later versions—the literate amateur clearly does not have the hands-on touch of the master cook [Martino]." In fact, Platina does little to improve Martino's recipes.

In addition to Martino as a source, Platina consulted Pliny the Elder, the Roman encyclopedist and author of *Historia naturalis* (*Natural History*), published in A.D. 77. *Natural History* is composed of thirty-seven books including all that the Romans knew about the natural world in the fields of botany, cosmology, astronomy, geography, zoology, mineralogy, medicine, metallurgy, and agriculture. Most of Platina's information on plants and animals comes directly from Pliny, including esoteric information on poisonous honey, the ancients using sugar only as a medicine, snakes rubbing their heads on fennel stalks to improve their eyesight, a rooster that conversed with Roman consuls, men sailing the Red Sea in boats made of single tortoise shells, and moray eels "driven to rage" by the taste of vinegar.

Platina's book has ten chapters called "books" and begins not with food but one's living conditions. In "Choosing a Place to Live," he advises living far away from "swamps, stagnant pools and hot sulfur springs." In "How to Go to Bed," he warns that people with weak stomachs should sleep facedown, but others should sleep first on the right side, then on the left. He agrees with Hippocrates that "copulation is a sort of epilepsy which should neither be desired too much nor completely shunned, since it makes for procreation, by which the species of living beings are preserved."

PLATINA'S CAMELLINE SAUCE

Take three pieces of bread, toasted and soaked with red wine and pound with raisins. Then soak this in red wine, must, verjuice, or vinegar. Put in as much as you like of ground pepper, cinnamon, and cloves. When it has been passed through a sieve into a bowl, serve to your guests. It is easily digested, is nourishing, makes the body fat, stimulates passion, and helps the stomach and liver.

Throughout the book, Platina gives us history lessons in the form of anecdotes. For example, in writing about Leonardo's favorite fruit, the fig, Platina tells a fascinating story that is a worthy anecdote in a cookbook of any era:

> The anxious Cato brought its fruit into the Senate when he
> was seeking a third Punic War and badgering the senators,
> especially those who did not think it all the stuff of Roman
> virtue that Carthage be destroyed. As soon as he said, "How
> long do you think this fruit has been picked from its own tree?
> Since all agree that it is fresh, know that it was picked not
> three days ago at Carthage, so close is our enemy," at once the
> Third Punic War was launched, by which Carthage, once the
> rival of the Roman Empire, was destroyed.

Picture Leonardo reading this and learning that the fig, ever-present in his life and his fables, was the trigger for the Third Punic War! Books like this were for Leonardo movies, TV, and the Internet all rolled into one.

Platina delights in telling us every little detail about the plants and animals used as food. "The pig is surpassed by no other animal in fat," he writes. "Varro affirms that he saw a pig in Arcadia which not only could not get up because of its gross fatness but could not even drive away a mouse which had made a nest by nibbling its flesh and had borne baby mice."

He gives detailed descriptions of the ingredients and how some of them grow. In his description of date palms, he writes:

> A female tree is considered sterile without the male, which
> ought to be planted nearby; females immediately become sterile
> if the male is cut down. The fruit of palms, however, does not
> grow among the leaves, but rather among the rising branches.

PLATINA'S FRIED GOURD

Scrape off the skin of a gourd and cut it into thin pieces. Place in a pot with water and when it comes to a boil, transfer it from the pan to a board and let it dry off a little. Then, roll it in salt and some white flour, then fry it in oil. After it is fried and placed in a dish, cover it with garlic sauce and fennel blossoms and with bread crumbs soaked in verjuice, so that it seems thin rather than thick. Place this sauce through a strainer.

He includes detailed cooking techniques:

> Pine kernels eaten rather frequently with raisins are even be-lieved to excite hidden passion. They also have the same power when seasoned with sugar. The nobler and rich eat these often during Lent as the first and last course. Sugar is melted, and pine nuts are rolled in it with a scoop and are made into the shape of a pastille [lozenge-shaped]. Gold leaf is added to these, for magnificence, and I believe, for pleasure.

And of course, there is constant medical advice:

> Marjoram is more effective in medicine than in food, the culti-vated the same as the wild. Ground with white wine, it resists the poison of scorpions and spiders. It combats indigestion, and taken with warm water, it soothes griping of the stomach.

Many of his recipes sound delicious, like Kid in Garlic, which would fit into the twenty-first-century barbecue kitchen, complete with serving suggestions:

> On a spit over a fire, turn a whole kid, or a quarter, with bits of lard and cloves of peeled garlic stuck all around it. Moisten frequently, add sprigs of bay or rosemary, with the seasoning I shall now describe. With verjuice and rich sauce, mix two well-beaten egg yolks, two well-pounded cloves of garlic, a bit of saffron, and a little pepper and put it in a pan. Then, sprinkle it on the kid that is cooking, and when it is cooked, put it in a dish and pour in part of the sauce, then sprinkle with finely chopped parsley. This dish, well-cooked, should be eaten quickly so it does not get cold.

Platina ends his book on a positive note, writing that if you use "temperance, strength, moderation, and prudence," then "greed, ambition, womanizing, stubbornness, fondness for dainties, intoxication, impudence, deceit, crime, shameless conduct, rashness, need, madness and despair will not mar your right pleasure and best of good health." This philosophy is echoed by Leonardo—see chapter five.

PLATINA'S BITTER FRITTERS

Soak flour and leavening with bitter herbs, cut up fine, as night falls. In the morning put in dry figs, chopped, and raisins, and mix. This mixture should not be too thin. Fry in oil. Coat the cooked fritters with sugar and honey. They are not thought to be very nourishing, but they help the liver, drive swelling from the bowels, and consume phlegm.

A BOOK ON BANQUETS AND AN OPERA WITHOUT MUSIC

One of the earliest books to analyze regional Italian cuisine was *Commentario delle piu notabili e mostruose cose d'Italia e altri luoghi* (*Commentary on the Most Notable and Outlandish Things Found in Italy and Elsewhere*) by Milanese writer Ortensio Lando, first published in 1548. The book follows a fictional traveler heading northwest from southeastern Italy, who is served regional food by innkeepers along the way. In Sicily, he is served macaroni that is "usually cooked with fat capons and fresh cheeses, dripping all over with butter and milk"; in Sorrento, he eats "peaches delicious enough to raise the dead"; and he finds that the "magnificent city of Ferrara, which reigns supreme in the manufacture of cured sausages and in the preparations of greens, fruits, and root vegetables" also has "excellent shad and sturgeon."

In Ferrara, Cristoforo Messisbugo was the *scalco*, or steward, who orchestrated the feasts of Ercole I, the first duke to allow the public to watch his court feasts. Messisbugo was also a court palatine, or officer, and he held that role long after Ercole's death in 1534. Messisbugo's book, *Banchetti, composizioni di vivande e apparecchio generale*, or *Banquets*, was published posthumously in 1549. This book has the usual recipes for daily food of the court in its second part, but it also has descriptions of molds that were used to create pastries in the shapes of castles, eagles, and fleurs-de-lys, as

THE MEATS OF MESSISBUGO

Cristoforo Messisbugo, author of *Banchetti, composizioni di vivande e apparecchio generale*, or *Banquets* (1549), compiled a list of his favorite meats, most likely with his favorites at the top: "The ox, the cow, the calf, wild and domestic boar, stag, deer, roe buck, lamb, kid, suckling pig, hares, rabbits, dormice, peacocks, wild and domestic pheasants. Partridge, thrush, woodcock, ortolans, garden warblers, quails, turtle doves, ducklings, cranes, geese, bittern, herons, snipe, wild and domestic duck, plover, and other fowl. Fat, fleshy capons and hens of a similar kind, domestic doves, and wood pigeons."

well as descriptions in detail of fourteen banquets and suppers he staged. The first chapter is a compendium of everything needed to produce one of Ferrara's legendary banquets, from the décor and table ornaments to the music and entertainment to all the foodstuffs. As with the Sforza court when Leonardo was producing such events, which we will explore in detail later, the meal is just one part of the banquet.

"The great *scalco*," writes food historian Roy Strong, "emerges from his book as a man of wide culture, with a keen eye, a considerable esthetic taste and a genuine passion for music. In his own way he was a minor theatrical genius endowed with high organizational skills." A good *scalco* had to have the organizational ability to manage a large staff of workers and performers, the creative mind of a show producer, and the practical experience of managing money and resources.

In the great cookbook tradition of Maestro Martino and Platina (Bartolomeo Sacchi) comes arguably the most influential cook of the Renaissance, Bartolomeo Scappi. The two Bartolomeos are often confused because of the similarity of their names, and in fact, I found errors of identification in many of the books I consulted. Bartolomeo Scappi was the chef to Pope Pius IV and Pope Pius V, but little is known of his life other than that, including the years of his birth and death. We do know that in April 1536, seventeen years after Leonardo's death, Scappi organized a banquet in honor of Charles V while in the service of Cardinal Lorenzo Campeggi. Much later, in 1567, he organized a festive banquet to celebrate the first anniversary of the pontificate of Pius V.

Scappi is most famous for his book *Opera*. It was a breakthrough publication that covered in detail more than forty years of cooking at the most prestigious court in Europe. *Opera* consists of six books and more

FRITTERS WITH ELDERBERRY FLOWERS

This recipe is from Cristoforo Messisbugo, the scalco, *or steward, at the d'Este court in Renaissance Ferrara.*

Get four ounces of flour, three blocks of ricotta made that very day (or a pound of soft cheese), a pound and a half of grated cheese, three ounces of salted cheese, a quantity of yeast that's as large as half an egg, and crush everything together in the mortar. To this mixture add six beaten eggs, a glass of milk and three ounces of rose water. Blend well. If the mixture is too thick, dilute it with the right amount of milk. Add three ounces of raisins. In summer, you can also add an ounce of elderberry flowers as you crush the ingredients in the mortar. Now, using a spoon, make fritters that are large or small, as you like. Fry them in oil, or butter, or in three pounds of lard. When they are done, sprinkle them with three ounces of powdered sugar before serving.

than 1,000 recipes. The first book is a dialogue in classical form between the master cook and his apprentice and covers the subjects of the tasks of the cook, the organization of meals, the types of kitchenware, and the inspection and preservation of various foods. The remaining five books cover cattle, game, birds, fish, vegetables, and eggs, with information and recipes, much like Platina's work. Then he gives 113 seasonal menus from simple suppers to elaborate banquets and follows with books on the work of the pastry cook and food for the sick.

Renaissance chefs like Scappi believed that many medical conditions could be treated with various foods, and in this way they kept alive the tradition of utilizing spices both as a food and a medicine. It was the responsibility of the cook, like that of a doctor in many ways, to keep people healthy. Scappi also likened himself to a "judicious architect," who "building on his exact design, lays a strong foundation, and on that gives the world practical and marvelous things."

The most famous parts of *Opera* are the kitchen illustrations, which have been reproduced in most modern books on Renaissance cooking. Scappi was in charge of the Vatican kitchens and was the first chef to describe the modern kitchen of the time. The book contains elaborate copperplate engravings of utensils, tools, gadgets like a pasta cutter, and a state-of-the-art roasting spit.

The illustrations in *Opera* reveal how the food was prepared during the election of a pope—and because of the possibility of poisoning, the

Spoons for making fritters in Scappi's kitchen, c. 1570
Sunbelt Archives

TORTELLI WITH HERBS "ALLA LOMBARDA"

This recipe, from Bartolomeo Scappi, is a good example of a Renaissance Milanese pasta recipe. "Tortelli" are the same as "tortelloni," and similar recipes are in use today in Lombardy and Emilia-Romagna.

Take the greens of beets and spinach and chop them finely. Rinse the chopped greens several times in water, and then squeeze the water out. Braise the greens in fresh butter and add a handful of aromatic herbs such as parsley and thyme. Take this mixture off the fire and place it in an earthenware pot or one of tinned copper. Add grated Parmesan cheese and fresh ricotta cheese in equal amounts, and season with pepper, cinnamon, cloves, saffron, raisins, and beaten raw eggs. If the mixture is too runny, add some bread crumbs. If it's too dry, add some more butter. Take a sheet of dough made in the manner suggested in Chapter 177. Make small or large tortelli by placing the mixture on the dough and folding it over and squeezing the edges together. Cook them in a rich meat broth. Serve the tortelli topped with cheese, sugar, and cinnamon.

meal was a high-security operation. Each cardinal had his food prepared by a private cook. Scappi was involved in this procedure and describes it in detail in the book. "Food was transported in ornate containers decorated with the arms of each cardinal," writes Riley, "inspected by a team of four bishops, and then passed through a revolving turnstile into the conclave. The wines were clearly labeled and in glass containers. Whole pies or chickens were not allowed, and everything had to be carved or sliced." The reason for this was to remove possibly dangerous knives from the dining room where the bishops were in close proximity to the servers.

For culinary purposes, Scappi divides Italy into three parts: Lombardy (the Po Valley), the grand duchies and Rome, and "the Kingdom," meaning the south and Sicily. He focuses primarily on three cities, Milan, Rome, and Naples, but also shows that he is familiar with the cuisines of Venice, Florence, and Genoa. He was the first writer to compare and contrast the regional cuisines, and only one recipe among the hundreds in his book is defined as *all'italiana* (Italian-style): Pieces of Grayling in Broth, Italian-Style. Many of the recipes reflect Scappi's Lombard heritage, such as Lombard Soup and Lombard Rice, and stuffed dishes like meats, pies, and noodles are quite prevalent.

Fish dominate the Venetian-style recipes, like Small Stuffed Squid in Fish Broth, but there are also Braised Loin of Beef and Cinnamon Cakes. In Rome, Scappi's adopted hometown, there is a wide range of recipes, such as meat loaves, macaroni dishes, Roman-style cabbage, and fish pancakes. From Naples comes Puff Pastry Filled with Squab Meat and Cabbage Soup with Mortadella. Clearly, he understood Italian regional cuisines to be a city-based phenomenon and believed that his selected cities reflected the cooking of the entire regions where they were located because they were the centers of trading and food distributions.

Unlike the works of Martino or Platina, Bartolomeo Scappi's menus show us how salads and fruit were worked into the richer dishes during every course of a sumptuous banquet. They were designed to refresh the palate and soothe the heavily spiced meat and fish dishes.

Scappi also wrote extensively about marinades and Arabic pastry-making, and included 200 recipes for waffles, flaky pastries, and cakes called pizze. Other foreign dishes in *Opera* were Moorish couscous and trout *alla tedesca* (German-style).

After Scappi, the food writers of the post-Renaissance period shied away from trying to create a compendium of "national" recipe collections based upon the major food cities of the Italian peninsula and instead focused on single regions. For example, Giovan Battista Crisci published *Lucerna de corteggiani* (*The Courtiers' Oil Lamp*) in 1643 in Naples. This book is specifically about southern Italy and contains the first extensive list of food products from Naples through Calabria and down to Sicily, and its emphasis is on cheeses and fruits. The book is not concerned with the larger cities but rather the countryside and its villages. In fact, only one city—Naples, the kingdom's capital—is featured when Crisci discusses the south, and most of the list consists of documenting the locations for fruit, such as Amalfi for peaches, Moiano for apples, Somma for wild cherries, Capua for salted ricotta, and Aversa for fine mozzarellas.

The trend toward cookbooks specifically about regional cuisines was inspired by Scappi's *Opera* and its presentation of regional recipes, but the writers to come delved even more deeply into each region. Another writer with a fondness for southern Italy was Antonio Latini, who published a two-volume work titled *Lo scalco alla moderna, overo l'arte di ben disporre i conviti* (*The Modern Steward, or The Art of Organizing Banquets*) from 1692 through 1694 in Naples. The first volume is "a brief description of Naples" and concerns "edible fruits and other things of special and rare quality produced in different parts of the same kingdom." Each of the twelve provinces within the kingdom is discussed, along with the food specialties of the villages in the provinces. For example, Campania's villages supplied Naples with "exquisite fruit" from Poggio Reale, "famous peas, cardoons, artichokes, radishes, and horseradish" came from Chiari, "quantities of pheasants" and "fine veal" from Ischia and Capri, and "brain sausages" from Principato Ultra.

The works of Crisci and Latini capped off the marvelous cookbooks and other gastronomical literature of the Renaissance and immediate post-Renaissance in Italy. The last comprehensive recipe collection was that of Latini. From the end of the seventeenth century to the middle of the eighteenth century, there is a gap in the culinary literature. "This silence," note food historians Alberto Capatti and Massimo Montanari, "reflected the sense of cultural inferiority experienced by Italians when French cuisine began to dominate throughout Europe, and it proved to be long lasting." In its place was "a return to local tradition and oral transmission, which is the primary instrument of local heritage."

Omelette with Herbs and Cheese

Here is the modern version of an omelette recipe from both Martino and Platina. It is unique because of its similarity to a classic French omelette—cooked in butter but slightly runny in the center. If you can't locate chard, substitute another green or just use more spinach.

INGREDIENTS

6 large eggs
½ cup milk
¼ cup water
2 tablespoons Parmesan cheese, freshly grated
¼ cup butter
¼ cup chard, minced
¼ cup spinach, minced
¼ cup Italian parsley, minced
½ teaspoon fresh sage, minced
½ teaspoon fresh mint, minced
½ teaspoon fresh marjoram or oregano, minced
Salt, to taste

In a bowl, combine the eggs, milk, water, cheese, and a little salt and beat together with a whisk. Melt the butter in a large skillet, add the greens and herbs, and sauté for about 5 minutes, stirring often. Add the eggs, stir, and then allow to cook without stirring until the bottom is firm and golden. The top should remain soft. Fold the omelette over and immediately slide it onto a plate for serving.

YIELD: 2 to 4 servings

Leonardo's Favorite Dish
(Minestrone Toscano)

Several of Leonardo's biographers mention that his favorite food was a simple minestrone soup. This one is Minestrone Toscano, from da Vinci's early home in Florence. Serve this soup with rounds of toasted bread and a little olive oil for dipping. The pasta traditionally used is shaped like rice. You may substitute rice if you wish.

INGREDIENTS

9 cups water
1½ cups dried white beans
1 clove garlic, minced
½ onion, chopped
2 tablespoons tomato paste
1 stalk celery, chopped
1 carrot, peeled and chopped
½ head of cabbage, chopped
2 leeks, chopped
2 zucchini, chopped
1 sprig fresh basil, minced
1 whole clove
2 sprigs fresh rosemary, minced
½ cup risoni or orzo pasta
Salt, to taste

In a soup pot, bring the water to a boil. Add the beans and boil for 2 hours. Remove half the beans from the pot and pass them through a sieve held over the pot. Cover the pot and set aside.

In a large saucepan, heat the oil and sauté the garlic and onion over medium heat for 1 minute. Thin the tomato paste with 1 teaspoon water and add to the pan. Add the remaining ingredients plus the bean mixture and simmer, covered, for 30 minutes.

YIELD: 4 servings

Chicken Breasts Braised with Verjuice

Renaissance food expert Gillian Riley comments on this recipe from Maestro Martino's *Libro de arte coquinaria*: "One of the most delicious recipes in the manuscript; its simplicity typical of the new, light cuisine of the Renaissance: simple seasonings, fresh flavors, uncomplicated to cook." If you cannot find unripe grapes, use ripe ones but add ⅛ cup lemon juice to the recipe. (Verjuice is the juice of unripe grapes and is sour.) To make saffron powder, dry the strands in the microwave and grind them in a mortar.

INGREDIENTS

2 slices bacon
4 chicken breasts, deboned, skin removed
½ cup chicken stock
24 large red unripe grapes, cut in half, seeds removed
1 tablespoon Italian parsley, minced
1 teaspoon spearmint, minced
¼ teaspoon freshly ground black pepper
1 small pinch saffron powder

In a skillet, render the bacon and then remove the slices. Brown the breasts in the fat until golden, about 2 minutes per side. Drain the fat and add the chicken stock and the grapes. Cover and braise over low heat for about 20 minutes. Remove the lid, add the remaining ingredients, and serve.

YIELD: 4 servings

Roast Young Lamb with Saffron Sauce

Martino called for a "quarter of a kid" in this recipe, but a small leg of lamb will work well. "All the flesh of the kid is good boiled or roasted," he wrote, "but the saddle is best roasted." He also noted that the kid should be "eaten as hot as can be." Serve with risotto.

INGREDIENTS

1 small leg of lamb, about 3 pounds
2 ounces pork fatback or substitute bacon or pancetta, cut into
    small strips
6 cloves garlic, cut into slivers
1 cup chicken broth
Juice of ½ lemon
2 egg yolks
½ teaspoon powdered saffron (microwaved, then ground)
2 cloves garlic, minced
1 tablespoon Italian parsley, chopped
Salt, as needed

Preheat the oven to 400° F.

Poke slits in the lamb with the tip of a sharp knife and insert a strip of fatback and a sliver of garlic into each slit. Sprinkle salt over the lamb.

In a saucepan, combine the broth, lemon juice, egg yolks, and minced garlic, stir well, and simmer for 5 minutes.

Place the lamb in a roasting pan and pour the sauce over it. Roast for about 1½ hours, or until the internal temperature reaches 150° F, for medium rare. Baste with the sauce every 15 minutes during the roasting. Carve and serve the slices covered with any remaining sauce. You may have to add more broth and scrape the remaining sauce off the bottom of the roasting pan.

YIELD: 6 to 8 servings

Caliscioni
(Marzipan Sweetmeats)

Some food historians believe that this recipe is the precursor to the diamond-shaped almond cakes of the town of Aix-en-Provence, the Calissons d'Aix. Martino adds a decorative touch: "And if you have an elegantly carved wooden mold, press it onto their tops and they will be nicer to look at." Note: this recipe requires advance preparation.

INGREDIENTS

FOR THE FILLING:
2 cups unblanched almonds
½ cup rosewater
1½ cups sugar

FOR THE DOUGH:
½ cup flour
2 tablespoons superfine or caster sugar
1 pinch salt
2 to 3 tablespoons rose water

To make the filling, place the almonds in a bowl and pour boiling water over them to cover. After the water cools, pour it off and rinse the almonds several times. Soak the almonds overnight to loosen their skins.

The following day, remove the skins from the almonds and process them in a blender or food processor with the rose water and sugar until smooth.

Preheat the oven to 250° F.

To make the dough, combine the flour, sugar, salt, and enough rose water to make a dough that does not stick to your fingers. Place the dough in plastic wrap and let sit for an hour.

Roll out the dough as thinly as possible on a lightly floured surface. Using a knife, cut the dough into 2-inch squares. In the center of each square, place a scant tablespoon of the filling and, using a dull knife, spread the filling over the dough square. Transfer the squares to a nonstick baking pan and bake for 1 hour. The result should be dry squares that are only slightly golden.

YIELD: about 25 *caliscioni*

Chapter Three

INVASION OF THE FOREIGN CROPS

From medieval times through the Renaissance, non-native foodstuffs were introduced into Italy, forever changing the cuisines of the various regions of Italy. The Arabs imported many of these new crops, and some were of minor importance, like taro, mango, bananas, and plantains. Among the significant vegetables introduced were spinach and eggplant, with the latter celebrated in Sicily in the dish *caponata*. New fruits included sour oranges, lemons, and limes, which are grown in the south in Calabria and in Sicily. Sorghum was initially important but was eventually supplanted by maize—see chapter seven for that story.

But the most significant new crops by far were rice, durum wheat, and sugarcane.

RICE BECOMES RISOTTO

Rice became an important nonmeat food in Europe throughout the Renaissance. The Moors first brought rice to Spain and planted it in Andalusia in the eighth or ninth century, and from there it was transferred to Sicily, possibly in the tenth century, where it was first sold only in spice shops. It was served in broth only to sick people, and a classic rice cure called for it to be cooked in a broth of goat's feet with almond milk and sugar added. The doctors changed their minds in the early 1500s and allowed healthy people to eat rice, but it was used primarily ground up as a flour to thicken soups.

THE ARABIAN INFLUENCE

"The Arabs certainly contributed to the development of medieval European culture, while the classical tradition clearly provided its foundation. This is true for gastronomy and even more so for dietetics, which developed during the Middle Ages on the basis of classical authors mediated by Arab writers and doctors. The two sciences shared the same basic interests. Spices, for example, made food more flavorsome and also more digestible."

—Massimo Montanari

"An enormous variety of new crops were discovered or diffused by the Arabs. These new crops played a central role in a more productive agriculture and were closely linked to important changes in the economy at large. The Arabs introduced higher yielding new crops and better varieties of older ones such as cabbage, increasing the productivity of land and labor."

—Clifford Wright

Then, in the late fifteenth and early sixteenth centuries, the grains themselves were used, and rice became a very popular food for the masses. In 1475, the duke of Milan, Galeazzo Maria Sforza, sent a sack of rice to the Duke d'Este in Ferrara, accompanied by a letter noting that a sack of seed would produce twelve sacks of edible rice grains. This correspondence indicates that rice had been planted around Milan for quite some time, but that rice cultivation might have been a noble concept in Ferrara. Galeazzo's successor and Leonardo's sponsor, Ludovico Sforza, further encouraged the planting of rice in Milan.

Martino's 1465 cookbook has several recipes for it, including Rice in Meat Broth, Rice Fritters, and Rice in Almond Milk. These recipes mark the first time that the use of whole grains is described instead of just rice flour. In addition to those recipes, Martino's contemporary, Platina, offers Rice Pie and makes this observation about the grain: "Rice is of a warm and dry force, and for this reason it is very nourishing, especially if it has been seasoned with ground almonds, milk, and sugar."

Rice was not an important part of court banquets and seems to have been used mostly to alleviate starvation among the peasant class. Often, rations of rice—up to four ounces per person per day—were issued by government authorities. This usage, combined with worries that flooding

Oryza sativa L.

Rice soon became a major foodstuff, especially in northern Italy.
Sunbelt Archives

RICE IN ALMOND MILK

This recipe from the early Renaissance chef Maestro Martino utilizes two of the most recent additions to Italian cookery—rice and sugar.

To make ten servings, take a pound of almonds and shell and skin them carefully so that they are white. Take half a pound of rice and wash it two or three times in warm water, then put on the fire in a pot with fresh water and cook it well. Take the rice off the fire, drain it, and let it dry. Pound the almonds thoroughly, sprinkling them with cold water frequently to prevent them from getting oily, thin with more fresh water, and pass through a sieve. Put this almond milk in a pot with half a pound of fine sugar; when it comes to a boil add the rice and let it cook over the coals, away from the flames, for half an hour, stirring often to prevent burning. You can cook the rice with goat's or other milk.

the rice fields was "unhealthy and pestilence-ridden," caused the grain to be excluded from recipe collections of the sixteenth century. In 1590, an ordinance in Lombardy sought to end the use of child labor in the rice fields, and rice usage virtually disappeared in seventeenth-century Italy, only to rebound in the eighteenth century (along with maize and potatoes) because of famine.

ON RICE

"Then we [in Italy] have rice, which is eaten in many countries but grown in few. We plant it in low-lying places, under water. It has a good yield, and is a most useful crop. It is a good food for the able-bodied, but hard to digest."

—Giacomo Castelvetro, 1614

Originally, just one variety of rice was grown, "Nostrale," but in 1839 a Dominican friar, Father Calleri, illegally imported forty-three types of Chinese rice from the Philippines and launched the beginning of the search for disease-resistant varieties. In 1856, a rice-processing factory was established in Genoa that later became the producer of the Riso Gallo brand, the leading rice brand now in Italy. Today Italy produces 1.3 million metric tons of rice, making the country Europe's largest producer. Of that production, less than half is consumed in Italy, and the rest is exported, mostly to European Union countries.

In his notebooks, Leonardo had several drawings of channels designed to drain the marshlands of the Po River plains for the planting of rice. The eminent Piedmont count, Camillo Cavour, recommended building a canal from the Po River and Lake Maggiore to irrigate rice fields in Vercelli, Alessandria, Pavia, and Novara. The canal was eventually built and is called Cavour Canal.

The Italians have a saying: "Rice is born in water but dies in wine"—probably an allusion to the process of adding wine to broth used to make *risotto alla Milanese*. One of the great culinary mysteries is how such a lowly grain as rice rose to eminence with the creation of dishes that are now regarded as masterpieces of Italian cuisine: the risottos of Milan and *risi e bisi* (rice and peas), the classic dish of Venice. Probably, given enough time, inventive cooks can make masterpieces out of the most basic foodstuffs.

CLASSIC RISOTTO ALLA MILANESE, VERSION I

"An onion, chopped and pureed, fried in butter until it is the color of a hazelnut, *cervellato* [a type of sausage], a good consommé, a little meat juice, let it boil for half an hour and pass the broth through a strainer; in this broth put rice and saffron; cook it until the rice is dry; put in plenty of *grana* cheese [similar to Parmesan], a little pepper and a lot of fresh butter."

—from *La cuciniera che insegna il buon gusto a cucinare alla casalinga*, 1809

The food historian Waverly Root mysteriously gives the date of 1574 for the invention of *risotto alla Milanese*, perhaps the most famous risotto of all Italian rice dishes. He quotes the description of Edouard de Pomiane, the late French doctor-biologist of the Pasteur Institute: "They bring you at dusk a preparation which seems to you to be made of grains of gold, and you are delighted already by nothing more than the sight of those grains of rice, each one distinct, each one gilded." The gilt is provided by saffron, part of the Italian Renaissance spice heritage.

The mystery of the date is cleared up by Italian food expert Anna Del Conte, who relates the legend that in 1574, the daughter of the craftsman who was making the stained glass windows for the Duomo in Milan was getting married. It was a custom of the time to add saffron to the molten glass to color it golden, and one of the apprentices had the idea to color the wedding feast risotto golden because gold was believed to have health-giving properties. It's a nice legend, but many food historians believe that *risotto alla Milanese* simply evolved from a Sicilian risotto that also used saffron. Another theory holds that risotto is just a simplified version of Spanish *paella*, which also contains saffron.

Another famous rice dish, *risi e bisi*, is such a part of the cuisine of Venice that Root claims that "only Venetian cooks can succeed in capturing the delicate springtime essence of this dish." In fact, the dish is always served on April 25, the Feast Day of San Marco, the patron saint of Venice. "To make it well," directs Giuseppe Mazzotti, an Italian gastronomic writer, "you must follow all the rules, especially this one: the peas must be fresh, sweet, and tender, shelled at the last minute." Anna Del Conte describes *risi e bisi* as "a very thick soup or a rather runny risotto," but also says that it "is the most aristocratic of all rice dishes."

CLASSIC RISOTTO ALLA MILANESE, VERSION 2

"Put a finely chopped small onion in butter, add marrow and butter in proportion, and when the onion has taken on a good golden color without browning, put in the rice and simmer until it has absorbed all the liquid. Then add the *cervellato* and immediately the boiling consommé. When it is two-thirds cooked, color it with the saffron dissolved in the consommé; and put in a little mushroom or truffle cut in slices, mix in at the same time some good cheese, and finish the cooking."

—From *Il cuoco senza pretese*, 1826

There are four basic types of Venetian rice: *ordinario*, a short, round grain used in puddings; *semifino*, another round rice used in soups and salads; *fino*, a long grain rice for risottos; and *superfino* (also known as *aborio*), a very long grain rice that is supposedly the best for risottos. And there are a huge number of rice dishes from Venice, which is not surprising since that city for centuries controlled the valley of the Po River, which is the largest rice-producing area in Italy. Rice with seafood is very common, and the grains are combined with eel, sole, fresh anchovies, shrimp, mussels, clams, lobsters, oysters, octopus ink, and even frogs' legs. Rice is also combined with mushrooms, cabbage, potatoes, beans, asparagus, spinach, and even grapes. Meats combined with rice include mutton, lamb, beef, veal, chicken livers, stewed chicken, and quail. Interestingly, *The Great Italian Cookbook*, compiled by the Italian Academy of Cookery and published in 1987, contains forty-five rice recipes and only sixteen pizza recipes.

RISI E BISI
(Rice and Peas)

"You prepare a *soffritto* with oil, butter, and chopped celery (there are those who add garlic, onions, and parsley; but the taste of celery must predominate); when it is browned, put in the rice. You boil the peas separately, to give flavor to the water. Moisten the rice with this water and a few tablespoons of beef and chicken bouillon. After seven or eight minutes' cooking, add the peas, stirring them until the rice has finished cooking. Two minutes before the end, add grated Parmesan cheese, and serve with solicitude."

—Giuseppe Mazzotti, quoted by Waverly Root in *The Food of Italy*

Waverly Root chronicles twenty-four rice dishes from Lombardy and notes "they are not *all* the Lombardy rice dishes. Some of the more interesting ones are *ris e corada*, rice boiled in consommé with calf's lungs; *risotto al salto*, leftover rice made into cakes and fried in butter; *ris e lentigg*, rice boiled in water with celery, onions, and lentils; and *risotto alla certosina*, with crayfish, mushrooms, and peas."

But rice has not been not so popular everywhere in Italy since the Renaissance. In a survey published in *Bollettino Doxa* in June 1950, for example, 35 percent of the people questioned in Sicily said they eat rice "rarely or never," while that figure for Piedmont was 10 percent. One respondent from Catania commented, "After eating a plate of rice, I feel I could immediately start on the pasta."

Macaroni Matters

The fresh pastas described by Martino and Platina in chapter one were probably made from soft wheat, or bread wheat, known botanically as *Triticum aestivum*. It wasn't until the introduction of hard wheat, *Triticum turgidum var. durum*, into Italy that *pasta secca* (dried pasta, or macaroni) could be made. This is because the hard wheat, or durum, or semolina wheat has a high gluten content but low moisture, ensuring that the pasta won't stretch or break during the drying process and that it will retain its shape and texture better during the cooking process.

In his discussion of the invention of macaroni in *A Mediterranean Feast*, Clifford Wright notes that it is of historical importance to know who invented macaroni for three reasons: famines could be reduced because dried pasta had a long shelf life; dried pasta could be warehoused to offset years of low food production; and the production of products such as *pasta secca* and hardtack (ship's biscuits) made long sea voyages possible, thus opening up the Renaissance world to exploration.

Wright quickly dismisses pretenders to the invention of macaroni, namely the Chinese. "Did Marco Polo bring back macaroni from Italy?" he asks. "Did he bring back a hard wheat dried pasta?" The answer to both questions is no. Marco Polo encountered a food made from a starchy flour, probably breadfruit or sago flour. Yes, he described this food in pasta terms he already knew, like *vermicelli* and *lasagne*, but in no case does he describe dried pasta, with which he was already familiar. So if the Chinese didn't invent macaroni, who did? Wright maintains that it was the Arabs. "The earliest evidence of a true macaroni," he theorizes, "occurs at the juncture

A wine lunch while harvesting wheat, c. 1590
North Wind Picture Archives

ODE TO MACARONI

Beautiful and white
As you emerge in groups
Out of the machine
If on a cloth
You are made to lie
You look to me like the milky way.

Zounds!
Great Desire,
Master of this earthly life,
I waste away,
I faint from the wish
To taste you
O maccheroni!

—Filippo Sagruttendio, from "Le laude de li maccarune"
("Praise to Macaroni"), 1646

of medieval Sicilian, Italian, and Arab cultures." The theory holds that the nomadic Arabs needed a portable food that was light, nourishing, and filling, and thus they invented pasta, possibly after some of them inhabited Sicily, where wheat was grown.

In the middle of the twelfth century, the Arab geographer Idrisi, writing about Sicily, commented on pasta-making there. "To the west of Termini, there is a town called Trabia, an enchanting place to live, abounding in streams that drive numerous mills," he wrote. "Trabia sits in a vast plain with many large estates, where great quantities of pasta are made and exported everywhere, especially to Calabria and other Muslim and Christian lands: many shiploads are sent."

IMPORTANT DATES IN THE HISTORY OF RENAISSANCE PASTA

1509: The vice-king of Naples proclaims, "When flour must be rationed for war, famine, and other such circumstances, retailers must not bake sweets nor must they manufacture macaroni or vermicelli, except in cases of illness."

1537: The "pasta miracle" occurs when a woman attempts to ridicule the friar Guglielmo Cuffitella by handing him a bowl of lasagne stuffed with bran, which miraculously turns into ricotta cheese as the friar eats it.

1548: Cristoforo Messisbugo advises that any cook in Naples should have dried pasta on hand at all times because it is an essential ingredient.

1570: According to Bartolomeo Scappi, a kitchen must have a kneading trough because it is an indispensable tool for making several kinds of pastas.

1608: A Roman law requires that bakers who intend to sell vermicelli must belong to the Guild of Vermicellari.

1639: Another Roman law forbids bakers from making vermicelli.

Around the same time, there were commercial contracts between Sicily and Genoa during the years 1157 to 1160 that prove that Sicilian macaroni was being imported into Genoa. Boccaccio (1313–1375) describes both macaroni and ravioli in his *Decameron*, and by the time of Martino, Wright suggests that "macaroni was a commonly known, if not commonly eaten, food in Italy."

One of *pasta secca*'s incarnations was lasagne, and the first written recipe for that dish appears in the fourteenth-century manuscript from Naples

A pasta cutter from Scappi's kitchen, c. 1570
Sunbelt Archives

called *Liber de coquina* (*Book of Cooking*). Sheets of pasta are boiled and then layered with spices (probably including sugar) and grated cheese. Other forms of *pasta secca* were little balls of pasta that would cook quickly in areas where firewood was scarce. Wright speculates that this pasta was made to resemble other grain foods that the Arabs were accustomed to, like barley and rice. His theory could account for the invention of the "soup pastas" such as *risoni* and *orzi*.

Of course, as is always true with historical theories, there are dissenters. Silvano Serventi and Francoise Sabban, authors of *Pasta: The Story of a Universal Food*, state: "Nowadays it seems difficult to attribute full credit for the invention of pasta to the Arabs, but this does not mean that they played no role in the spread of certain types of pasta products." They point out that making pasta requires access to hard wheat flour, which in turn requires regular wheat harvest and milling equipment, which the once-nomadic Arabs lacked, at least until they inhabited Sicily.

PAOLO ZACCHIA'S PASTA SOUPS

The following description of the "lean dishes" of pasta soups appeared in Paolo Zacchia's Vitto quaresimale (Food for Lent) *in 1636:*

"They are varied, depending on whether the pastas are fresh or dried, narrow or broad, or made with wheat flour or other ingredients. They have many varied shapes, and some are round, like vermicelli and macaroni, and some of the round ones are hollow. Some pastas are broad and flat, like lasagne, while some small and round, like the kind called *millefanti*. There are also pastas that are narrow and flat, like *fettuce*, which are usually called *tagliolini*, and other short and thick, called *agnolini*. Others are fatter and longer and are called *gnocci*. And they exist in a thousand other guises, none of them any better than the others."

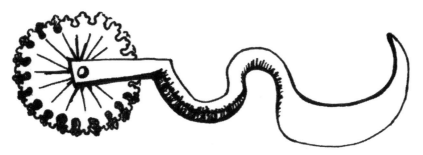

Another pasta cutter from Scappi's kitchen, c. 1570
Sunbelt Archives

As to the question of why the Greeks and Romans did not invent hard wheat pasta, Serventi and Sabban propose that in the Mediterranean region there were two fundamental cereal-based dishes: a kneaded dough that was always cooked with dry heat (namely, bread) and gruel or polenta that was cooked by boiling in moist heat. They state: "Pasta products were unthinkable, because they straddled both categories and therefore belonged to neither: they were made of a kneaded dough, like unleavened bread, but, in common with gruel cereals, were cooked in moist heat." Wright has a much simpler answer to the question: There is no evidence that the Greeks, Romans, or even the Etruscans grew durum wheat, so they didn't have the one necessary ingredient to make macaroni.

AL DENTE

Meaning "to the tooth," *al dente* is the expression for pasta that's removed from the cooking before it gets soft, with some firmness remaining. Cooking pasta this way is such a universal culinary custom that many people assume that it has been around as long as pasta itself, but this is not the case. The tradition of cooking pasta with its nerve, or *nerbo*, intact, as the Neopolitans say, dates only from the early years of the twentieth century—although it was derived from the culture of centuries of cooking dried pasta.

By the time of Maestro Martino, who was the chef at the Sforza court at Milan prior to Leonardo da Vinci's arrival, there were numerous variations on pasta, using both bread wheat and durum wheat. His Roman-Style Macaroni was a typical fresh pasta that would be called fettuccine today:

> Take really good-quality flour, sift, and make the pasta a bit
> thicker than you would for lasagne. Roll it around the rolling
> pin, take the pin out, and cut the pasta up into strips the
> width of your little finger, which will look like ribbons or
> laces. Cook in rich broth or water, which should be boiling
> when you put them in.

Another of his fresh pastas was Ravioli for Meat Days, which was stuffed with meat and cheese:

> For ten servings take half a pound of hard cheese and a little
> soft cheese. Cook a pound of pork belly or a calf's head until
> tender. Then pound it well and add some finely chopped
> sweet herbs, pepper, cloves, and ginger; a capon's breast, also
> pounded, would be even better. Mix all these with the chees-
> es. Then roll out your pasta very thin, and enclose portions
> of the mixture in it in the usual way. These ravioli should not
> be more than half the size of a chestnut. Cook them in good
> capon or meat broth colored with saffron.

Martino also gave recipes for two dried pastas. The first he called Sicilian Macaroni, which implies the durum wheat connection with Sicily. This is the classic Renaissance macaroni that has been passed down to this day:

> Take best-quality flour and work it with egg whites and rose
> water or ordinary water. For two serving dishes you will not
> need more than one or two egg whites. Make the pasta very
> stiff, then make little strips a hand's-breadth long and as thin
> as a straw; take a thin iron rod a hand's-breadth or more long,
> and lay it on the strip of pasta, rolling it with both hands over
> the tabletop, then draw out the rod and you will have your
> macaroni with a hole through them. They should dry out
> in the sun, and will keep for two or three years, especially if
> made in the month of August.

Although Martino mentions lasagne several times, he does not have a specific recipe using it as a main ingredient. Instead, the dried sheets are used as a cover, or thick topping for tarts, so they won't dry out: "When it seems to you to be almost done, cover the top with a thick layer of dried-out sheets of lasagne, and leave it to cook a little more."

Making pasta in Naples, c. 1880
North Wind Picture Archives

THE ORIGIN OF TORTELLINI?

Tortellini, the famous stuffed pasta from Bologna, was supposedly invented by a cook who molded the pasta in the navel of his lover. Hard to believe? Try this one: The goddess Venus, in the disguise of a human woman, visited an inn in Castelfranco. The cook was fortunate enough to be passing by her room and through the door that was ajar caught a glimpse of her in the nude. He was, of course, inspired to create a pasta in the shape of her navel. The love of tortellini in Bologna is beyond reason: "It is more essential than the sun for Sunday," wrote one impassioned journalist, "or love for a woman."

As we can see from the sophistication of Martino's recipes, pasta had achieved a presence in Italian cooking by the middle of the fifteenth century. This was the beginning of the formation of pasta as a culinary category, not just another starch on the menu or a side dish. Note that during the early Renaissance times, dried pasta was quite expensive, about twice the cost of meat, and though they could afford it, the court chefs of the time, like Martino, preferred to make their own. The reason for this was probably that Martino distrusted preserved food prepared by others outside of his kitchen. In the words of Guglielmino Prato, a grocer from Asti at the turn of the seventeenth century, "It is customary to purchase *fidelini* made by pasta makers, with the considerable risk of finding that they have been made with very low-quality materials or made with old or spoilt flours, especially during famines, and that is why sensible gentlemen will have the *fidelini* made by his servants."

The small middle-class population, such as merchants, probably purchased the dried pasta, and it evolved into a mainstay of the Italian menu. Like rice was eventually elevated from a dish for peasants to the risottos we know today, similarly pasta fed both the commoner and the courtier. In this case, however, pasta was a side dish for the aristocrats and a main dish for the masses.

THE PASTA REVOLT

In 1647, the people of Bari in Apulia revolted against their Spanish rulers because of pasta! The Spanish, always interested in increasing state revenue through taxation, decided to tax flour. At first the Apulians accepted the tax, but when Spanish soldiers began entering the kitchens of citizens to measure their flour used in pasta and bread, enough was enough. The fighting in the streets lasted about a week, and then the Spanish authorities gave in and repealed the tax. "It has been suggested plausibly," writes Waverly Root, "that the men of Bari were defending not only their pasta, but also their women. Spanish soldiers had a reputation for gallantry, and when they invaded the family kitchens, it appears the flour was not always the only thing they inspected."

In addition to the *pasta secca* available, there were also fresh pasta shops to meet the local demand, particularly in northern Italy. These pasta makers were called *lasagnari*, and in some cities there were enough of them around to form a guild. For example, in Florence in 1311, the *lasagnari* and the cooks joined forces to form the *Arte dei Cuochi e Lasagnari*, or the Guild of Cooks and Lasagne Makers. Similar guilds were formed in Genoa, Perugia, and Milan. The governments of the cities with such guilds regulated the prices charged for pasta to prevent fraud and price gouging, and the prices were public by proclamation. A magistrate could impose fines on violators of the pasta ordinances.

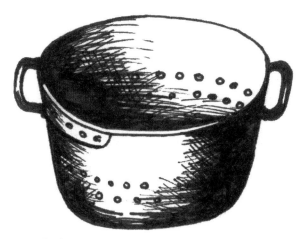

Colander for draining pasta from Scappi's kitchen, c. 1570
Sunbelt Archives

Later, in 1546, the Neapolitan Corporation of Spaghetti Makers and the Neapolitan Corporation of the Macaroni were formed. Only a few years later, in 1570, Bartolomeo Scappi, the "secret chef" of Pope Pius V, published his *Opera* that further promoted pasta. Scappi gave recipes for *millefanti*, which was millet-sized grains of pasta that were stored in small bags, and he also wrote about *maccheroni a ferro*, which was sweetened with sugar and colored with saffron. *Tortelli con polpa di cappone* was pasta stuffed with breast of capon.

SCAPPI'S PASTA

In his *Opera*, Bartolomeo Scappi recorded many recipes for and with pasta:

- *Millefanti*, small pasta "grains" made from semolina and warm water that are dried in the sun and stored in small bags.
- *Maccheroni a ferro*, long strips of flattened dough made with sweetened dough colored with saffron.
- *Maccheroni detta gnocchi*, a pasta shaped by pressing the dough with the fingers across the back of a grater, a tradition still in practice today in Veneto.
- *Tortelli con polpa di cappone*, Tortelli with Ground Capon Meat.
- *Tortelletti con pancia di porco*, Tortellini with Pork Belly (Bacon).

Scappi also promoted the use of the kneading trough, sometimes called a pasta brake, which was a machine with a lever that went up and down, striking the dough and effectively kneading it. Another recommended machine, the *ingegno*, was a press that used dies to extrude the dough in various pasta shapes.

By 1610, stuffed pastas and the techniques for making them were even more in vogue. The musician and scholar Giovanni del Turco was also interested in pasta, and in his early sixteenth-century book, *Epulario e segreti vari: trattati cucina toscana nella Firenze seicentesca*, he gives instructions for making *agnellotti in minestra*, tortelli stuffed with meat that were as large as walnuts. The meat "must be wrapped in a sheet of pasta as thin as the one used for lasagne," he writes. To stuff it, a pocket must be made: "All the pasta that extends here and there must be pushed upward, leaving a small box in the middle."

One of the more notable additions to pasta literature was a poem by Count Francesco de Lemene, "Della discendenza e nobilta de maccherone in modena," published in 1654, which not only attempted to classify pasta types but also provided a "genealogy" of macaroni:

> Pasta was born of flour. Prolific mother who, as widow, gave birth to a natural son called Gnocco (who did not have a happy ending), and who had already had other children from her three husbands, Canella [rolling pin], Kneading Trough, and Press. With Canella, she had produced Polenta and Lasagna, the latter then becoming the mother of Cake and Raviolo. But the most wonderful offspring, Maccherone, was produced with Press. The descendant of Maccherone is Fidelino, the father of Pestarino.

In 1699 the Guild of Vermicellari in Naples changed its name to the Guild of Maccaronari, which indicates that the term "macaroni" was generic, referring to all types of pasta, both those worked by a press and a die and those made by hand. And the term was not exclusive to Italy. In England, in the early 1700s, the term "macarone" came to mean a rich person who could afford to buy exotic foods—a kind of snob. There was a Macaroni Club in London that catered to young, educated, and wealthy men who appreciated good food served in spectacular fashion.

Scappi's outdoor kitchen, c. 1570
Sunbelt Archives

TOP FIVE MOST INTERESTING
PASTA SHAPES

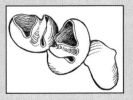

Lumachi or **lumaconi**—snail-shaped pasta shells, for stuffing; shown is Conchiglioni

Stelline—little stars for soup

Fusilli Stretti—corkscrews for thick, chunky sauces

Orsetti—pasta bears for kids

Farfalle—bowties or butterflies for creamy sauces

PASTA IN NAPLES, 1787

"The macaroni, the dough of which is made from a very fine flour, kneaded into various shapes and then boiled, can be bought everywhere and in all the shops for very little money. As a rule, it is simply cooked in water and seasoned with grated cheese."

—Johann Wolfgang von Goethe, *Italian Journey*

The first American pasta connection occurred in 1789, when Thomas Jefferson requested that his friend, William Short, buy a pasta machine for him in Naples. In a letter dated February 11, Short writes to Jefferson explaining that he had purchased the machine, but that it was much smaller than those used in pasta factories. It was a small press made for home use, and perhaps it made the trip back to Virginia. But if it did, it could not meet the needs of Monticello; just six months before he died, Jefferson authorized the purchase of 112 pounds of macaroni.

By this time, pasta factories were springing up all over Italy. In 1812, the area around Savona and Porta had 148 such establishments, and Genoa had 250. Genoa exported the pasta to Cyprus, Egypt, France, England, Spain, and North and South America. Increased mechanization provided the means to produce more pasta, and the first hydraulic pasta press was introduced in the 1850s, followed by steam mills and mixers, and in 1882, the first hydraulic press with a vertical cylinder. The first industrial pasta factory in the U.S. was built in Brooklyn in 1848 by a Frenchman, who spread his spaghetti strands on the roof to dry in the sunshine.

MAKING PASTA IN ITALY, 1830

"When the dough has been sufficiently kneaded, it is squeezed, through the simple application of pressure, through a number of circular apertures the dimensions of which determine the name of the pasta that issues forth. The ones with a larger diameter produce macaroni, the ones with a smaller diameter, vermicelli, and the smallest diameter, *fideline*."

—*Penny Magazine of the Society for the Diffusion of Useful Knowledge*, London

Recently, pasta took a tumble because of the low-carb diet fad, but seems to be resurgent. Americans consume about twenty pounds of pasta per year per capita. In Italy the amount is sixty pounds, an amount that hasn't varied much since 1954.

Sugar and Sweets

Sugar was one of the "spices" imported from the east by Arab caravans to Alexandria and then moved in small quantities throughout Europe by Venetians, who controlled the spice trade in pre-Renaissance times. The Venetians included sugar as one of their spices imported from India by way of Alexandria from as early as the tenth century, and one scholar claims that it first reached Venice in 996—but that date may be late.

Wherever the Arabs went, they brought the technology for growing and processing sugar with them. Sugar, history holds, followed the Qur'an. The Arabs adopted, and introduced into other countries, a number of irrigation devices, including the Persian bucket wheel, the water screw, and the *qanat*, a series of gravity-assisted underground tunnels that carried ground water to the cane fields.

Despite the increase in sugar

The introduction of sugarcane revolutionized Italian sweets and desserts.

North Wind Picture Archives

production by the Arabs, it took centuries for sugar to arrive in other parts of Europe: England in the late twelfth century, Denmark in 1374, and Sweden in 1390. By 1243, Henry III of England was able to purchase 300 pounds of lump sugar, and, as if to prove how much the British royalty appreciated it, in 1287, during the reign of Edward I, the king's household used 677 pounds of regular sugar, 300 pounds of violet sugar, and 1,900 pounds of rose sugar. The latter were sugars colored with violets and roses. In 1288, the total sugar consumption of the royal household shot up to 6,258 pounds.

In Italy, Venice first imported processed sugar from Alexandria in a variety of forms. A commercial manual compiled in Florence between 1315 and 1340 by Francesco Balducci Pegolotti reveals that sugar was available in loaves, candied, refined, and colored by violets or roses. By the fifteenth century, however, Venice was buying sugarcane and producing sugar in its own refineries, along with molasses, and by the sixteenth century, Naples was consuming an astonishing 1,500 tons of sugar per year.

One of the reasons for the increasing sugar consumption in Europe was the invention of the vertical three-roller mill, which crushed the cane for its juice. The mill was powered by water, people, or a combination of animals and people. One source attributes this invention to Pietro Speciale, the prefect of Sicily in 1449, but others insist that the mill was a much later invention that was invented in the New World and brought to the Mediterranean in the early 1600s.

Gradually, sugar replaced honey in Italian cooking from the early fifteenth century on, and by the middle of that century it was common everywhere—among the upper classes, of course. It achieved a remarkable reputation, and one early Italian writer, Costanzo Felici, noted:

> Sugar is an excellent accompaniment to everything, or one
> could make it such. As the saying goes, "Sugar never spoils
> a soup." It makes eating more refined, and very frequently,
> drinking also, by rendering both experiences sweet and flavor-
> ful, and human nature finds great pleasure and delight in its
> sweet flavor.

Pasta recipes appearing in Renaissance cookbooks often called for a topping of cheese, sugar, and cinnamon; recipes for cooking ham and salami called for them to be boiled in milk with two pounds of sugar for every eight pounds of meat. Sugar was often mentioned as an alternative to other spices, and it appeared in spice mixtures called "Venetian spices," along with cinnamon, cloves, nutmeg, Guinea pepper, and saffron. Often, dishes sweetened with sugar were served at the beginning of the meal. Sugar was often used in sauces as well; one Venetian sweet and sour sauce that was a flavoring for roasts of all kinds called for spices, sugar, and vinegar. During the early Renaissance, sugar was a characteristic trait of Italian cooking, while bitter flavors were preferred in France, and the Germans continued to use honey.

Sugar is used liberally in Martino's recipes from the mid-fifteenth century. One sauce for chicken calls for bitter orange juice, rose water, sugar, and cinnamon, while a recipe for a "white dish" serving twelve that contains goat's milk, rice flour, and a capon's breast requires an astonishing pound of sugar, and the result is sprinkled with even more sugar. Another white dish with fish calls for a half pound each of ginger and sugar. Green beans and squash were cooked with sugar and cinnamon, and a dish of hemp seeds requires a pound of them, a pound of almonds, and a half-pound of sugar.

Martino's recipe for Marzipan Tart calls for a pound each of sugar and almonds, and then before serving, the tart is sprinkled with rose water and powdered sugar. (See the recipe in the preceding chapter.) Martino was one of the first cooks to use sugar in large quantities to make dishes that are specifically sweet, such as fritters, sauces, and tarts, rather than using sugar as a seasoning like salt, in the medieval manner.

Platina also liked sugar and wrote an essay about it, saying that "[i]ts

CATALAN MIRRAUSTE

Maestro Martino proves that sugar can be added to virtually any recipe. The word mirrauste *comes from the Catalan region and means "half-roasted."*

First take pigeons, chickens, or capons and prepare them for roasting. Put them to roast on the spit, and when half cooked take them off and divide them into quarters. Then cut each quarter into four pieces and put them in a pot. Take some almonds toasted over hot coals and rub with a cloth to remove the skins, then pound them. Next take two or three slices of lightly toasted bread, and three or four egg yolks and pound them with the almonds. Dilute this mixture with good vinegar and broth and push it through a sieve over the meat in the pot, adding some mild spices, ginger, plenty of cinnamon, and a lot of sugar. Next put the pot over the coals and let it simmer for a good hour, stirring all the while with a spoon. When cooked send this *mirrauste*, as we call it, to the table in serving dishes, or rather bowls, which would be more suitable.

force is warm and damp so that it is of good nourishment, is good for the stomach, and soothes whatever discomforts there are, if any." He notes, "For nothing given to us to eat is so flavorless that sugar does not season it. Hence arose the saying of frequent use: 'No kind of food is made more tasteless by adding sugar. The quality of sugar almost crosses over into the qualities of those things to which it clings in the preparation.'"

Most of the recipes in Bartolomeo Scappi's *Opera* call for sugar, continuing the tradition of the earlier Renaissance cookbook authors. The worship of sugar continued in the elaborate banquets described in chapter six, where artistic sculptures were made entirely out of sugar. And even wine was not immune to the charms of sweetness, as demonstrated by the words of Maestro Morando, a poet of the time:

> Glorious, sweet wine
> Makes a man plump and fleshy
> And lightens his heart.

During the time of the Renaissance, sugar (and specifically sucrose) had five main uses: as medicine, spice or condiment, decorative material, sweetener, and preservative. These uses often overlapped, which was part of sugar's charm. For example, sugar used to coat medicines was being used as both a preservative and a medicine; sugar used to preserve fruits was both a preservative and a sweetener; and when sugar was used to make a sculpture, it was usually eaten after it was displayed. However, sugar would not be considered a food until the late eighteenth century, by which time it had completely saturated popular cooking.

As a medicine, sugar's value was touted by the Arabs first, and then as usual, claims to its healthful qualities were adopted by Europeans. Today, this seems ironic because of the widespread theories of the supposed "dietary evils" of sugar, but the fact remains that it was one of the most important medical ingredients in the medieval Arabian apothecary. Sugar was prescribed in the form of syrups (*shurba* in Arabic); robs, which were an infusion of flower petals into sugar water; and other sugar-based "medicines" including decoctions, infusions, powders, and the entire range of medicinal compounds. These sweet combinations were used as a treatment for a wide range of maladies, including fever, coughs, stomach diseases, and even chapped lips. After the transfer of these beliefs to Europeans, the phrase "like an apothecary without sugar" came to mean a state of utter desperation or hopelessness.

The sixteenth-century herbalist Jacob Dietrich, who used the improbable pen name Tabernaemontanus, detailed the medicinal qualities of sugar while, in balance, detailing its effects on the teeth:

> Nice white sugar from Madeira or the Canaries, when taken moderately, cleans the blood, strengthens body and mind, especially chest, lungs, and throat, but it is bad for hot and bilious people, for it easily turns into bile, also makes the teeth blunt and makes them decay. As a powder it is good for the eyes, as a smoke it is good for the common cold, as flour sprinkled on wounds it heals them.

The use of sugar as a decorative material began with the Arabs, who combined it with almonds to make marzipan, which could be molded much like clay. Other malleable combinations included sugar with the oil of almonds, rice, scented waters, and various gums. Artworks from the sugar bakers were a tradition in upper-class Arabian culture. One report noted that a sultan in Egypt used 73,300 kilograms of sugar during Ramadan to make sculptures, including a large tree. Another traveler reported that around 1400, a mosque was built entirely of sugar and that after the festivities concluded, beggars were allowed to eat it minaret by minaret.

SCAPPI'S BRANCHED FRITTERS

In a bowl, combine eight ounces of flour with ten fresh eggs, three ounces of melted butter, two ounces of sugar, a little saffron, a pinch of salt, and two ounces of rose water. Beat the mixture very well. Heat lard in a frying pan until very hot. Place the batter into a spoon with holes and use a spoon without holes to force the batter through, and make it spread everywhere, so that the branches of batter cover the bottom of the pan. When you see that the batter has made a "flower," turn it once so that it doesn't brown too much, and then remove it, because this batter cooks very quickly. Repeat the process, and put one "flower" on top of the other and powder them all over with sugar. They will keep in a warm oven when covered with a piece of paper.

Such practices were transferred to the courts of Renaissance Europe, and confectioners practiced their art from Italy to England. They combined sugar with oil, crushed nuts like almonds, and vegetable gums to make a very plastic, claylike substance that could be molded into any conceivable form, and then either baked their sculptures or simply allowed them to dry. In England, the displays of sugar sculptures were called "subtleties," and they were made to represent animals, buildings, or even message-carrying objects to further political aims. Thus sugar, beyond its intrinsic value, was a substance that could be sculpted, written upon, admired, read, and then eaten!

Between 1573 and 1584, several editions of John Partridge's *The Treasurie of Commodious Conceites, and Hidden Secrets* was published in London, and Partridge's recipe for marchpane (marzipan) was set into history:

> Take...blanched almonds...white sugar...Rosewater...and Damask water.... Beate the Almondes with a little of the same water, and grind them until they be small; set them on a few coales of fyre, till they waxe thicke, then beat them again with the sugar, fine...mix the sweet waters and them together, and...fashion your Marchpane.... Set it upon a warm hearth...and ye maye while it is moyshe stiche it full of Comfets, of sundrie colours. If it be thorough dried, a Marchpane will last many yeares.

Sugar and sweetened dishes were only available to the upper classes during the Renaissance, and the writer Gentile Sermini, who lived in the early part of the fifteenth century, urged the cook to: "Make sure that the peasant does not taste sweetness but only sour things. Rustic he is; rustic he will remain." Thus sugar became a symbol of courtly cooking and refinement, and it remained out of the reach of the commoner for centuries—until production radically increased.

It was Portugal that ended the Venetian sugar monopoly, under the direction of Prince Henry the Navigator. Prince Henry was a Portuguese royal prince, soldier, and patron of explorers who sent expeditions to Africa and the Madeira Islands. He directed Portuguese adventurers to take sugarcane from Sicily and plant it in the Madeira Islands from 1418 to 1425, and he financed the construction of the first water mill to crush the cane and extract the juice in 1452. Lisbon began importing sugar from these islands and became the sugar capital of Europe in the sixteenth century. In 1498, sugar exports from Madeira were 1,700 tons, and of that amount, 183 tons went to Genoa, 211 tons to Venice, 85 tons to Livorno, and 29 tons to Rome.

As a sign of Portuguese sugar dominance, even the Florentine traders gradually switched suppliers from the Venetians to the Portuguese by the beginning of the sixteenth century. But despite the change in suppliers, the discovery of the New World brought sugarcane to the Caribbean and sugar back to Europe, with the first sugar grown in the New World presented to Spain's Carlos I in 1516. By 1580, the Sicilian sugar industry could only supply the local market, and exportation dwindled to nothing because of the competition of New World sugar and its increasing consumption and uses.

Perhaps it seems odd to think of sugar as a preservative like salt, but in reality it has many of the same properties, namely the ability to draw off moisture and deprive bacteria of the water and oxygen they need to survive. So sugar is a good medium for the suspension of fruits, vegetables, and even meats to seal them off from the environment that would cause them to spoil.

And of course, the sugar experts, the Arabs, made the first such discoveries as early as the ninth century, when documentation of sugar preservatives in the form of syrups, fruit preserves, and candied capers first appeared. In the *Compendium aromatariorum* (1488), Saladin d'Asculo describes how concentrated solutions of sucrose could prevent fermentation, and how a thick coating of powdered sugar could preserve dairy products. During this time, besides drying, the only practical way to preserve fruits was to boil them in syrup and flavor them with spices and more sugar, gradually replacing the water with sucrose. This practice led to candied fruits, which have a particularly long history in both Italian and British cuisines. Henry IV's wedding feast in 1403 offered sugar plums, sugared roses, and comfitures of fruit and many spices, including ginger, cardamom, anise, cinnamon, and powdered saffron.

From such culinary experimentation, a candied fruit tradition has lasted for centuries, such as fruitcake in England and candied fruits in Italy. Waverly Root notes that "frutta candita," Sicily's famed candied fruit, can include "oranges, lemons, figs, pears, cherries and even squash" and that the candied fruit makers of that island "claim to have mastered the technique of making them so that the flavor of the fresh fruit remains unaltered in the candied form." The candied fruits are enjoyed in their own pure form, but are also added to nougat, marzipan, pastries, creams, and ice cream.

FRUTTA CANDITA

"The fruit most commonly candied are mandarins, figs, plums, pears, and apricots. They are first cooked very lightly in order to open the pores and allow the sugar to be absorbed more easily, then boiled in syrup. During the boiling, the water evaporates and when the syrup has reached the right degree of sugar content the heat is turned off. The fruit, which has absorbed the sugar while releasing some of its juices, is left in the syrup for three to six months, or—ideally—one year. It is then ready to be candied by dipping it into crack-boiled sugar. Candied fruit should be eaten within one month if wrapped; if loose it should be eaten within a week. If kept longer it tends to become dry."

—Anna Del Conte, *Gastronomy of Italy*

The food historian Elizabeth David writes that the candied fruit makers in northern Italy have also mastered the art. "Italian preserved and candied fruit is spectacular," she notes. "Whole pineapples, melons, citrons, oranges, figs, apricots, red and green plums, pears, even bananas in their skins, are sugared in the most skilful way, and make marvelous displays in the shops of Genoa and Milan."

Another of the great Italian sugar legacies is *cassata*, a Sicilian dessert that is made with sponge cake (more properly, an egg cake known as *pan de spagna*) combined with ricotta, lots of sugar, and candied fruits. It is thought to be of Arab origin, but in Italian hands it was transformed into an Easter specialty that was considered to be so tempting and decadent that it was banned in 1574. The diocese of Mazara del Vallo prohibited the nuns from making *cassata* at the monastery during the Holy Week because the nuns preferred preparing it to attending to their vows.

"Renaissance cooking became a triumph of sugar," observe food historians Capatti and Montanari, but the trend would not end there. Its use was extended to the present day in Italy, as we shall discover in chapter seven.

Rice, durum wheat, and sugar forever changed Italian cuisine. Rice and the pasta made from the wheat eased the threat of famine, while sugar provided needed calories. The three of them helped set the stage for the elaborate banquets of the Italian Renaissance and the Italian cuisine that would follow.

Sicilian Caponata
(Eggplant Relish)

Eggplants were introduced into Sicily by the Arabs, and despite being a member of the nightshade family, they had time to become familiar to the population and were adopted into Sicilian cuisine. This relish, served over pita triangles or garlic toast, can be a throwback to more ancient times by substituting powdered almonds for the tomatoes. Sometimes a light dusting of unsweetened cocoa powder is added to this recipe.

INGREDIENTS

1½ pounds eggplant, cut into ¾-inch cubes, skin left on
¼ cup olive oil
4 inner celery stalks, chopped
1 onion, finely sliced
6 ounces canned tomatoes, minced
1 tablespoon sugar
½ cup red wine vinegar
½ cup capers
½ cup green olives, sliced
Salt, as needed

Place the eggplant cubes on paper towels and sprinkle them with salt all over. Allow to sit for 1 hour, then, using other paper towels, dry them off.

Heat the oil in a skillet until hot but not smoking and sauté the eggplant cubes until golden brown. Remove and drain on paper towels. Add the chopped celery and fry it in the same oil until it is golden, then remove and drain on paper towels. Repeat with the onion until it is soft, then add the tomato. Cook for about 10 minutes, stirring frequently.

In a saucepan, combine the sugar and vinegar and heat them. Add the capers and olives and simmer for about 10 minutes. Add in the eggplant, celery, and onion/tomato mixture. Simmer for 5 minutes, then remove from the heat and allow to stand for about an hour. Serve at room temperature.

YIELD: 6 to 8 servings as an appetizer

Risi e Bisi
(Rice and Peas)

Here is one of Venice's favorite dishes that is served on St. Mark's Day, when the young peas are just ready in the garden. The texture of the dish should be somewhere between a soup and a risotto—just thick enough to be eaten with a fork.

INGREDIENTS

½ pound peas in the pods
5 cups chicken stock
2 tablespoons butter
1 medium onion, finely chopped
2 tablespoons parsley, minced
4 slices prosciutto, cut into strips
1 cup long grain rice
¼ cup grated Parmesan cheese
Salt and freshly ground black pepper, to taste

Shell the peas and reserve the peas and the pods. Wash the pods and combine them with the chicken stock in a pan. Simmer for 15 minutes, then strain the pods, reserving the broth and discarding the pods.

Heat the butter in a large saucepan and sauté the onion for about 5 minutes. Add the parsley and prosciutto and sauté for 5 minutes, stirring often. Add the rice and peas and cook for 2 minutes, then add the chicken stock. Bring to a boil, then reduce the heat and simmer, uncovered, for about 25 minutes, stirring occasionally. Add salt and pepper to taste. Remove from the heat, stir in the cheese, and serve.

YIELD: 4 servings

Fettuccine di Basilico
(Pasta with Basil Pesto)

Although it is difficult for us to imagine Italian food without tomatoes, many of its most delicious dishes hail from Renaissance time or earlier, before they were introduced to Europe from the New World. This is a classic pasta that Leonardo might have eaten with one of his salads.

INGREDIENTS

2 ounces fresh basil leaves
½ cup extra virgin olive oil
2 tablespoons pine nuts
2 cloves garlic, peeled
½ cup grated Parmigiano-Reggiano cheese
2 tablespoons grated Pecorino Romano cheese
1 pound fettuccine, cooked al dente
3 tablespoons butter, softened to room temperature
Salt, to taste

Place the basil leaves, olive oil, pine nuts, garlic, and salt in a blender and process until the mixture is almost creamy. Remove to a bowl and stir in the cheeses. Toss the fettuccine with this mixture and the butter.

YIELD: 4 servings

Cassata Siciliana

Gastronome Renato Giani called this intensely sugared dish one of "the two unshakable rocks of Sicilian desserts," with the other being cannoli. It is traditionally served at Easter feasts, and an old proverb says, "No one can be without *cassata* on Easter."

INGREDIENTS

1 large sponge cake, thinly sliced
¼ cup marsala
1½ cups ricotta cheese
⅔ cup caster sugar
4 drops vanilla extract
2 ounces candied fruit, finely chopped
2 ounces candied orange peel, chopped
2 ounces semisweet chocolate, grated
3 cups confectioners' sugar
4 drops green food coloring
3 tablespoons water
½ cup whole mixed glacé fruits

Line the sides and bottom of an 8-inch mold with aluminum foil, then line it with sponge cake slices, reserving some to cover the top. Sprinkle with half the marsala.

In a blender, combine the ricotta, caster sugar, and vanilla and blend on low. Add the candied fruit, candied peel, and the chocolate and mix until well-blended.

Add this mixture to the mold, cover with the remaining slices of sponge cake, and sprinkle with the remaining marsala. Cover the mold with aluminum foil, press down on the molded ingredients, and refrigerate for 3 hours.

In a double boiler, melt the confectioners' sugar and add the food coloring and water. Stir well with a wooden spoon and take care that it does not brown. Unmold the cassata and cover with the icing and the glacé fruits. Slice thinly and serve.

YIELD: 8 servings

Malmona
(Orange-Flavored Rice Pudding)

This recipe from Tuscany incorporates several of the foods introduced into Italy by the Arabs: rice, sugar, and citrus.

INGREDIENTS

1½ cups sugar
6 tablespoons all-purpose flour
½ teaspoon salt
2 cups whole milk
2 cups cream
2 cups cooked rice
3 tablespoons frozen orange juice concentrate

Mix together the sugar, flour, and salt in a saucepan. Set the pan over a high heat and add the milk and cream while stirring constantly. When the mixture is hot, add the cooked rice and the orange juice concentrate. Keep stirring as it comes to a boil, then reduce the heat slightly to keep a rolling boil and stir for 3 minutes. Then remove it from the heat and allow to cool. It thickens as it cools.

YIELD: 6 to 8 dessert servings

Chapter Four

How to Cook for the Pope

Given the conveniences now present in home kitchens for preparing our modest feasts, it is difficult to imagine the challenges faced by the chefs of the Renaissance as they prepared banquets with dozens of courses for sometimes hundreds of people. We take for granted basic things like a constant source of heat, running water, and numerous machines that ease our work.

But in the Renaissance kitchen, how was the fire kept stoked? How was the water supplied? How were the pots and utensils cleaned? How was the spit kept constantly turning? The banquet preparation was an enormous effort that involved a team of people who not only worked together but also lived together.

As glorious as the triumphs of the Renaissance kitchens were, they had modest beginnings.

From Lowly Hearth to the Duke's Kitchen

Archaeological excavations of late medieval dwellings in coastal France have revealed quite a difference in the "kitchens" of the peasants and the wealthy. In the one-room, primitive cottages, there was usually a single hearth, but never a fireplace. This is primitive cookery, akin today to grilling meats in the same storage shed you sleep in. However, some of the tools used were not so primitive.

The most common archaeological find in excavations of late medieval and early Renaissance common houses is ceramic cookware, but it is rarely mentioned in the history books. These ceramics were part of the "majolica" tradition of pottery that dated from the island of Majorca prior

Positioning the pot in the Scappi kitchen, c. 1570
Sunbelt Archives

to the thirteenth century, when it was transferred to the Italian ports of Genoa and Pisa. Plates and vases were used in the home not only for cooking and eating but also for storing foods and liquids. They were long-necked bulbous pots, convex vessels with small handles, vials, and medicinal jars that were ideal for storing medicines, spices, balsams, and oils. Larger items included round pots for cooking and round pots with beaks for pouring and transporting liquids, especially water. Eventually, the more common uses for majolica evolved, and their style became associated with coveted objets d'art.

Other cooking equipment in the modest kitchens included iron skillets, copper pots and kettles, and saucepans. Mortars were found in these kitchens as well, but grills and spits were found almost exclusively in the kitchens of the wealthy, as were molds for tarts, waffle irons, and griddles.

Wood played a substantial and often underestimated role in the preparation and preservation of food. It was used to make salt cellars and salting tubs, vinegar storage bottles, water pails, cookie cutters, kneading boards, sieves, cheese boxes, oven paddles, pot covers, bowls, ladles, and stirring spoons. Some of the other kitchen gadgets of the time included copper measuring cups, tin strainers, cheese graters, perforated spoons, and iron meat hooks.

In the kitchens of the bourgeois, the housewife, working with her daughters, would have to master more techniques than a modern cook. Besides the actual cooking, she would be in charge of the household supplies of wood and water and would have to maintain the fire in the hearth. The food historian Odile Redon adds: "And no one paid her overtime when, knife in hand, she disjointed or boned a chicken she had just plucked, or skinned a hare or an eel, or emptied and cleaned a length of entrails, or scalded a piglet to remove the fine hairs from its skin."

In the homes of the wealthy, there was a room devoted to cooking with a large rectangular hearth that was six feet long and lined with bricks. In towns, the homes of the wealthier people often had ovens for baking bread, yet another step up in the development of the kitchen. Contrast these with the communal ovens used by the common folk. Of course, the best kitchens, those of the court castles, were often housed in a separate structure devoted just to food preparation.

In the main kitchen area, the windows were built high on the walls to provide maximum light and ventilation. The fireplaces were wide and shallow and had a chimney to draw off most of the smoke, and the floors were usually stone or paved tiles. There was shelving on the walls, a sink, and large chopping blocks. Illustrations of some of these kitchens show cats on mice-catching duty but, as today, they were also pets attracted to the aromas of food being cooked.

The better kitchens had two separate pantries, one for the storage of food items and wine (sometimes a cellar) and the other for large cooking pots, copper drinking cups, and pewter. Even in homes large enough to have a "dining room" equipped with its own table and chairs, the servants did not dine with their masters and spent much of their time in the kitchen.

AS THE SPIT TURNS

"The most basic method was to turn the spits by hand, a tiresome and very uncomfortable job due to the overpowering heat of the fire. A kitchen assistant known as a turnbroche or turnspit performed this task, but because the job was a tedious one, dogs and geese in treadmills were also frequently used to rotate the spits. In the sixteenth century, Doctor Caius, founder of Caius College, Cambridge, described the turnspit dog, a breed now extinct: 'There is comprehended under the curs of the coarsest kind a certain dog in kitchen service excellent. For when any meat is to be roasted, they go into a wheel, which they turning about with the weight of their bodies, so diligently look to their business, that no drudge nor scullion can do the feat more cunningly.' An eighteenth century writer tells us that these unfortunate creatures frequently hid or ran away when there was any indication that a roast was about to be cooked. Geese were said to be able to keep the spits turning for up to twelve hours at a time."

—from HistoricFood.com

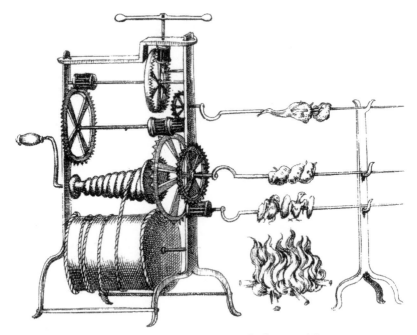

Tri-spit for roasting from Scappi's kitchen, c. 1570
Sunbelt Archives

The main cooking techniques used in the early Renaissance were roasting, which was done on spits or grates over an open flame or hot coals; boiling in large cauldrons; frying such foods as fritters or French toast; hearth baking when an oven wasn't available (braziers or covered pots were used); and baking, which was limited to professional bakers or manor kitchens.

One of the basic kitchen tools was the tin-lined copper pot, which was used for centuries for the basic task of cooking directly over flames or coals. The knives, spoons, forks, stands, trivets, and frying pans were usually iron. The rolling pins were made of wood, while the mortars were fashioned from bronze and marble.

The pope's chef, Bartolomeo Scappi, who compared himself to an architect, wrote about the operation of his large kitchen in 1570:

> While preparing a meal always required great stamina, the variety and organization of the tasks would vary greatly from place to place. In a team of cooks working in a royal or noble kitchen, the work was divided among specialists who were in

turn assisted by numerous obedient helpers: from the *hateur*, who was in charge of roasting, to the *potier*, who saw to the pots and dishes, everyone had his own job to attend to. The *saucier* simmered the sauces; the *potagier* peered into the pots of potage; the *broyeur* manned the mortar; and of course the *soffleur* fanned and maintained the fire.

Kitchen work was very labor-intensive, and it appears that as many as sixteen people worked in and around his kitchen. In addition to the team mentioned above, there were unskilled laborers to chop and haul wood for the fires, carry water for the pots, scrub the dirty cooking equipment, shape the pasta, knead the bread, sharpen the knives, serve the dishes in the dining area, pour the water and wine, clear the table, and wash the dishes and glasses. In addition to these cooks and workers, there were two other essential staff members, the butcher and the carver, and they were very different. According to Vincenzo Cervio, a carver who was also an author (*Il trinciante*), "This sort of cutting should not be called 'carving' nor should those who perform it be called 'Carvers.' We men of reason should call them 'butchers' or 'kitchen carvers.'" The butcher, symbolized by the meat cleaver, killed and bled the animals, skinned them, then cut the meat into roasts and chops. He dealt constantly with death and raw meat and was considered to be of low class. By contrast, the carver was received at court as one of "three honorable offices which great Princes usually appoint to care for the needs of their stomach: the Steward, the Cup-Bearer, and the Carver," in the words of Cervio. His work was not done in bloody slaughter rooms but rather in the banqueting hall, performing for the guests.

The noted Italian chef Giuliano Bugialli comments:

> The fine carving of fruit, vegetables, and meats for decoration and presentation had a very important part in the Italian Renaissance meal. No book has documented it better than *Il trinciante*, first printed in Venice in 1580. The volume details the carving and boning—the latter especially for rolling and stuffing—of every beast eaten, all carefully illustrated. It also includes decorative carving for presentation of fruit and fish. With page after page of drawings, *Il trinciante* offers amazing evidence of Italian Renaissance cuisine's highly ritualized sophistication.

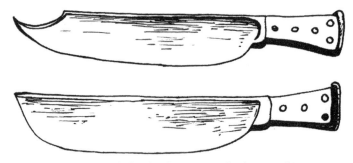

Cleavers for the butcher from Scappi's kitchen, c. 1570
Sunbelt Archives

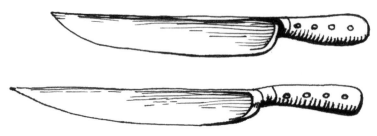

Knives for the carver from Scappi's kitchen, c. 1570
Sunbelt Archives

The carver's performance was carefully staged. The knives and forks he used—and only he could clean, polish, and sharpen them—were placed between two plates and covered with a folded napkin, as Cervio notes, "out of respect for the Prince, before whom no object can be placed without cover." The carver approached the table, taking care not to touch it with his body. He uncovered the knives with a flourish, placing the napkin over his left shoulder. Then he picked up the carving fork in his right hand and elegantly tossed it into his left hand, using his thumb, index, and middle fingers to keep the prongs in a vertical position. Next he lifted the carving knife, holding it not by the handle, but using his thumb and forefinger to grasp the blade near the handle where it was dull. Using the fork to raise the roast, he sliced off first wide, thin pieces and then smaller pieces, and they would fall on the plate set below the roast. Using just the point of the knife, he took salt from the cellar and sprinkled it around the edge of the plate. As the servers took the carved meat to the guests, the carver carefully cleaned the knife and fork with the napkin and then covered them with it, his show over.

And what dishes did Scappi serve Pope Pius V at the feast in 1567? The menu appeared in *La cucina*, by Vincenzo Campi.

First Course—Cold Delicacies from the Sideboard

- Pieces of marzipan and marzipan balls
- Neapolitan spice cakes
- Malaga wine and Pisan biscuits
- Plain pastries made with milk and eggs
- Spanish olives
- Prosciutto cooked in wine, sliced, and served with capers, grape pulp, and sugar
- Salted pork tongues cooked in wine and sliced
- Spit-roasted songbirds, cold, with their tongues sliced over them
- Sweet mustard

Second Course—Roasts

- Fried veal sweetbreads and liver, with a sauce of eggplant, salt, sugar, and pepper
- Spit-roasted skylarks with lemon sauce
- Spit-roasted quails with sliced eggplants
- Stuffed spit-roasted pigeons with sugar and capers sprinkled over them
- Spit-roasted rabbits with sauce and crushed pine nuts

SCAPPI'S SWEET MUSTARD

In the first course of Scappi's banquet for the pope, one of the dishes listed is Sweet Mustard. It seems a little odd for mustard to be included with the songbirds and pork tongues, but this is no ordinary mustard!

Take a pound of the sauce of grapes, and another sauce made of quinces cooked in wine and sugar, plus four ounces of apples cooked in wine and sugar, three ounces of candied peel of eggplant, two ounces of candied lemon peel, and half an ounce of candied sour orange peel, and grind all the candies together with the apples and quinces in a mortar. Pass this through a sieve together with the grape sauce, and add to this more or less than three ounces of mustard seed, depending on how strong you want it. And when it is mixed, add a little salt and sugar, half an ounce of cinnamon, and a quarter of an ounce of cloves. If you don't want to make a paste of the candies, then chop them finely. If you don't have sauce of grapes, substitute more quinces and apples cooked in the same manner.

- Partridges, larded and spit-roasted, served with lemon slices
- Pastries filled with minced veal sweetbreads and served with slices of prosciutto
- Strongly seasoned poultry with lemon slices and sugar
- Slices of veal, spit-roasted with a sauce made from the juices
- Leg of goat, spit-roasted with a sauce made from the juices
- Soup of almond cream, with the flesh of three pigeons for every two guests
- Squares of meat aspic

Third Course—Boiled Meats and Stews

- Stuffed fat geese, boiled Lombard-style and covered with sliced almonds, served with cheese, sugar, and cinnamon
- Stuffed breast of veal, boiled and garnished with flowers
- Milk calf, boiled and garnished with parsley
- Almonds in garlic sauce
- Turkish-style rice with milk, sprinkled with sugar and cinnamon
- Stewed pigeons with mortadella sausage and whole onions
- Cabbage soup with sausages
- Poultry pie with two chickens for each pie
- Fricasseed breast of goat dressed with fried onions
- Pie filled with custard cream
- Boiled calves' feet with cheese and egg

Fourth Course—Delicacies from the Sideboard

- Bean tarts
- Quince pastries with one quince in each
- Pear tarts wrapped in marzipan
- Parmesan cheese and Riviera cheese
- Fresh almonds on vine leaves
- Chestnuts roasted over the coals and served with salt, sugar, and pepper
- Milk curds with sugar
- Ring-shaped cakes
- Wafers

Here in 1567, sweets are being served lightly in the first course, assuming that marzipan has sugar in it, but they predominate in the last course, presaging a dessert course to finish the banquet.

PIE WITH A CHOICE OF THREE CHERRIES

Bartolomeo Scappi knew that different kinds of cherries ripened at different times, so he advised the cook to choose the right one for the time the pie is cooked. There is no recipe for the pie crust, but one was given in another part of the book. A testo was a tool for baking pies and cakes in the coals of a fire.

Cherries from Rome are better than the others, and begin to ripen at the end of April, and wild cherries ripen in mid-May, and in June the sour cherries ripen. Choose one or the other, using those that are not too ripe, and let them stew with fresh butter. Stew them enough that they will go through the sieve. Add with the sieved cherries fresh ricotta, some mozzarella, a little hard cheese, and Naples mostaccioli pasta ground into a powder. Add pepper, cinnamon, and beaten eggs to your taste. Place into a pie pan lined with pie crust, top with another pie crust. Cook it in the oven or underneath the "testo," making its icing with sugar and rose water and serve hot. One can cook strawberries this way, which start to ripen in May and are in season for all of June, but in Rome they start in April.

THE GUESTS AND THE FEAST

The location of the feast in a manor setting would be outdoors during warm weather, but in the winter, in a wealthy urban home, a trestle table would be set up close to a fireplace so that honored guests could be seated with their backs to the fire. They would sit either on chairs with high backs and armrests or on comfortable benches with backrests and pivoting seats that could be swiveled around to face the fire. Benches without backrests would be provided for the less important guests.

And that's what the feast was all about—it was an exercise in social standing. Such banquets were governed by strict protocol that determined the placement of the tables, the seating of the guests, and the quality of the food to be served. A central table was reserved for the host (duke, cardinal, or other nobleman). The more distinguished the guest, the closer he or she was placed to the host.

There is a fascinating story about this protocol by Giovanni Sercambi that involves the poet Dante, who was invited to a feast hosted by the king of Naples, Robert. Dante arrived poorly clothed, and because of his appearance, he was seated as far from the king as possible. He was hungry and ate anyway but left town immediately after dining. When the king heard about this incident, he was mortified and sent a messenger to invite

Scappi's prep kitchen, c. 1570
Sunbelt Archives

Dante back to the court. This time Dante arrived in beautiful clothes the king had sent, and he was seated "at the top of the first table, right next to his own." The service of the meal began, and Dante deliberately began spilling food and drink all over his clothes. The shocked king asked him why he was behaving in such a manner, and Dante replied:

> Your majesty, I know that in paying me this great honor you are in fact honoring my clothes, and I wanted those clothes to benefit from the food that is being served. And I shall tell you frankly that I had no less genius or common sense when I came the first time, when I was seated at the tail end of the table because I was poorly dressed. Here I am again, with the same degree of genius, but this time well-dressed, and you have had me seated at the top of the table.

As to the serving order of the dishes, the sixteenth-century poem "Il saporetto" by Simone Prudenzani of Ovieto describes it thusly:

> The meal begins with ravioli and lasagne in broth,
> and with soups described as in the French style;
> boiled meat and rich game stews come next, then
> roast game birds, followed by torte and other savory
> meat pies. Dried fruits and spices conclude the meal.

I should note here that I studied the menus of many feasts, and the order of the dishes varied enormously, with sweets at the beginning, middle, and end, interspersed as if they were the palate refreshers of the late twentieth century in the U.S. Generally speaking, the roasts and stews were served to the guests during the middle part of the banquet.

How were the guests eating? With fingers, knives, and spoons—and perhaps, in some cases, forks. The food historian Odile Redon and others have argued that forks were commonly used in homes and taverns in the late fourteenth century in Italy. But Roy Strong has another theory. He writes that forks were known in Rome but were a rarity during medieval times. But they made a comeback of sorts during the Renaissance—at least among the upper classes. In Botticelli's *The Wedding Feast* (1483), the ladies seated at the table on the left are using forks to eat dessert.

In 1492, Lorenzo de' Medici had eighteen forks for his dining room, so I agree with Roy Strong's observation: "It offered yet another opportunity

Serving the Scappi banquet, c. 1570
Sunbelt Archives

for the upper classes to distinguish themselves from the peasantry." But they were not common; Strong found a 1536 reference to them and not another one until 1563, again in a painting—this one by Paolo Veronese, *The Marriage at Cana*. Strong theorizes: "Evidence would suggest that initially they were used only for special foods like salads and sweetmeats, in particular for fruits in syrup." However, two-pronged forks were common in the kitchens. Bartolomeo Scappi's copperplate engravings in his *Opera* of the Vatican kitchens show just such a fork amidst illustrations of kitchen layouts, pots and pans, and numerous tools and gadgets, including a pasta cutter.

Producing the Banquets

Roy Strong, the author of *Feast: A History of Grand Eating*, wrote that banquets for the pope, or for any ruler for that matter, needed a talented person in charge:

> The greatest innovation, however, was the emergence of a new major court official to supervise all aspects of such events—the choice of location, the decoration of both room and table, the menu, the mechanics of food presentation and the selection of music and other forms of entertainment to enliven the meal. In Ferrara, this man was the *scalco* or steward.

Today the word "steward" conjures up a server, but in reality there is a far more formal meaning of the term. The first definition in the dictionary reads "A person put in charge of the affairs of a large household or estate, whose duties include supervision of the kitchen and servants." The *scalco* was in effect a producer of live entertainment events, and he had to have an eye for everything, including the shapes the napkins were folded into, the operation of the kitchen and servers, the music being performed, and selection of the performers. "The great *scalco*," writes Strong, "[is] a man of wide culture, with a keen eye, considerable aesthetic taste and a genuine passion for music."

THE POPE'S WINE

Pope Paul III (1468–1549) was a wine lover who had his own wine steward, Sante Lancerio, who served the pontiff *malvasia* for dipping his biscotti. According to Lancerio's memoirs, the wine was served to the pope sometimes "for the nourishment of his body" and "sometimes for gargling."

The Renaissance kitchen had a definite hierarchy of help who worked together to produce the elaborate banquets. At the top, as we have seen, was the *scalco*, or steward, who was in charge of not only the kitchen, but also the dining room. The dining room was supervised by the butler, who was in charge of the silverware and linen and also served the dishes that began and ended the banquet—the cold dishes, salads, cheeses, and fruit at the beginning and the sweets and confections at the end of the meal. The kitchen was supervised by the head cook, who directed the under-cooks, pastry cooks, and kitchen help.

During the serving of the main courses, with two to twenty dishes per course, another important part of the team was the carver, who cut the bread, meats, fish, and the rest of the foods consumed by the diners, adding salt and table seasonings as needed. The carver was in charge of the distribution of the main courses at the banquet table. When carving, say, roast fowl, he would raise the slices in the air in a ritual gesture and then arrange them on a platter in a circular pattern. The platter was then presented by servers to the guests, and the carved meat (and other dishes) was transferred to individual diners' plates. This serving was all within the context of elaborate table decorations. Italian cuisine experts Alberto Capatti and Massimo Montanari comment:

> The decorations of the table demanded architectural constructions, emblems, figures of sugar or butter molded in human and animal shapes, gigantic landscapes and volcanoes of pasta, and a profusion of natural and artificial flowers.... The display on the table... represented not only the prince's political dominion over the products of the land but also his symbolic power over terrestrial space, over history, myth, and all living creatures.

SUGAR SCULPTURES FOR THE POPE

"[There were brought forth] confectionery victuals, three of the Labors of Hercules, that is, the Lion, the Boar, and the Bull, and each one of them was in the shape of a common man. But first Hercules, nude, with the skin of a Nemean lion and with stars on his shoulder to signify holding up the Sky; and following the labors of Hercules, grand confectionery castles were brought forth complete with towers and fortifications inside, and an infinite number of confectioneries in all different manners; and these castles with confectioneries were plundered and tossed down from the tribunal into the square to impress those present; and it seemed a great storm. Then there was brought forth a large confectionery serpent on a mountain, very lifelike. And then a dish of wild men. Afterward, perhaps ten great ships with sails and ropes, all of them confectioneries and filled with nuggets of sugar. While still eating, there was also brought forth a Mountain, from which a man jumped out, who acted very impressed with the banquet, and he said some words, but not everyone understood them."

—Bernardino Corio, c. 1500

This elaborate decoration and serving was what in restaurants is called "the front of the house." In "the back of the house," primarily the kitchen, the head cook was dealing with not only the preparation of the dishes but the supervision and discipline of his staff. Drunkenness was a big problem, then as now, in large kitchens. The Florentine cook Domenico Romoli advised: "Above all do not mingle with drunkards even if they are the most accomplished masters of cooking you can find, for having imbibed before preparing the food, they are themselves cooked before the appetizer."

Another big problem in the Renaissance kitchen was fighting dirt, and the need for cleanliness led to traditions of correct attire for the kitchen help, including the kitchen whites, which would quickly reveal the parts of the kitchen and the pots and pans that were unclean.

Discipline in the kitchen was very important to prevent drinking, theft, contamination of food, or, worse yet, outright attempts at poisoning the guests. Firewood was stolen and sold by the help, apprentices regularly helped themselves to leftovers, and unless the head cook was constantly watching—assuming he himself was honest—the kitchen would be plundered. Since the steward was ultimately responsible to the lord of the house, it was his responsibility to limit the thievery but at the same time

Scappi's main kitchen, c. 1570
Sunbelt Archives

preserve the in-kind gratuities that were given to the cooks, apprentices, and other kitchen help like the dishwashers.

When the team coordinated well together, excellence was the result, from modest banquets to very elaborate ones. Renaissance food expert Gillian Riley describes one of the more casual feasts:

> The pope's banquet, held after Vespers on Friday the 31st day of May (the day of Venus) in a garden in Trastevere was a modest little supper for a few friends—about forty of them—with only three courses. The first course offered twenty-six items, from dressed anchovies to fresh strawberries and clotted cream with sugar. The second course was of twenty-four dishes including tender young broad beans in their pods (probably eaten raw with salt), baby artichokes cooked in butter with bitter orange juice and pepper, bite-sized chunks of Parmesan cheese, and fresh green almonds, split and served on vine leaves. The third and final course had eighty-eight bowls and one hundred and twenty-eight dishes filled with candied fruits, preserves, sugared almonds and pine kernels, and boxes of quince paste. The meal was completed with perfumed toothpicks and, for each guest, a posy of silk flowers with golden stems.

The chronicler Claudio Benporat, writing around 1500, describes one of the more elaborate banquets for the pope:

> The banquet...took place in a great hall [in the cardinal's residence at Piazza Santi Apostoli] where there was a sideboard with twelve shelves on which gem-studded trays of silver and gold were featured. Two tables covered by four tablecloths were prepared in the middle of the hall: the first was for the seven nobles of the highest station while the other table was for the lesser among them. In accordance with the custom of usage since the beginning of the century, the guests were still standing when they were served a meal that included trays of candied fruit covered with gold leaves and accompanied by painted glasses of *malvasia*. Once the guests were seated, musicians with horns and pipes announced the next dishes, which were divided into four services in correspondence with the four tablecloths that covered the tables. The first service combined pork livers, blancmange, meats with relish, tortes and pies, salt-cured

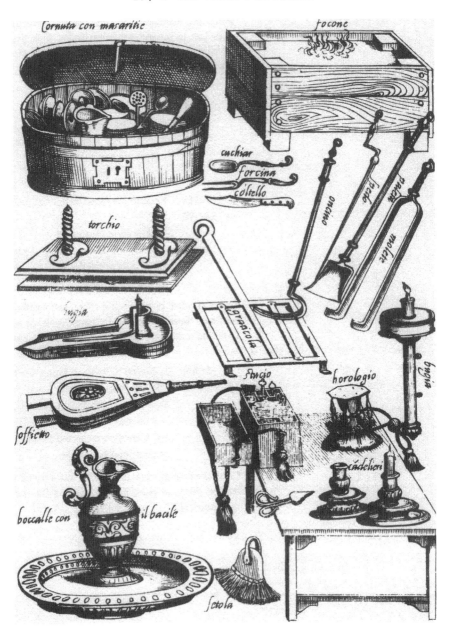

Scappi's kitchen gadgets, c. 1570
Sunbelt Archives

pork loin and sausage, roast veal, kid, squab, chicken, rabbit, whole roasted large game, and fowl dressed in their skin or feathers. [This was just the first service.]

Within the context of the pomp and circumstance associated with papal banquets, the pope was the honored guest, so we might expect that he would sit at the head of the main table. But at the banquet given to celebrate the consecration of a new pope in Rome, the new pontiff was led to a separate table by two cardinals. The pope-elect took his seat and ate alone.

THE POPE'S FISH

"Besides the trout of the mountain streams, Umbria enjoys many other fish from lakes Trasimeno and Piediluco, especially the former. Trasimeno's great delicacy is the lasca, the European roach, considered so great a delicacy that ever since the Middle Ages it has been sent to Rome for the Pope's Easter Dinner."

—Waverly Root

Passato di Spinaci alla Nocciole
(Spinach Soup with Hazelnuts)

"Hazelnuts are good to eat both green and dried. We keep the dried ones for eating in winter and during Lent," wrote Giacomo Castelvetro in 1614. Indeed, this soup combining hazelnuts with spinach would make a perfect dish to serve to the pope on lean days.

INGREDIENTS

2½ pounds fresh spinach
Water, as needed
2 tablespoons butter at room temperature
¼ cup flour
1 cup half and half
5 cups chicken stock
1 teaspoon freshly grated nutmeg
¾ cup peeled hazelnuts, oven-roasted and coarsely chopped

Heat a large amount of salted water until it boils. Add the spinach and cook for 3 minutes. Drain and place the spinach in ice-cold water. Drain again and place in the blender or food processor until smooth.

In a large saucepan, melt the butter over medium heat, add the flour, and stir until well-blended. Stirring constantly, add the half and half until smooth. Add the pureed spinach, stirring constantly, then add the chicken stock and nutmeg. Simmer the soup for about 5 minutes, stirring occasionally. Serve with the chopped hazelnuts sprinkled on top.

YIELD: 6 servings

Bruschetta and Pine Nut-Stuffed Game Hens

In the tradition of Scappi's spit-roasted birds served to the pope, here is a modern interpretation. You can certainly use the spit on your grill if you have one, or the hens can be roasted in the oven. Serve this with a simple soup-and-salad combination.

INGREDIENTS

4 slices Italian bread, grilled or toasted, and cut into croutons
2 cloves garlic, chopped
¼ cup pine nuts, chopped
1 teaspoon Italian parsley, minced
1 teaspoon sage, minced
½ teaspoon salt
⅓ cup olive oil
2 Cornish game hens, rinsed and dried
½ cup chicken stock
Juice of ¼ lemon

Preheat the oven to 450° F if using it.

In a bowl, combine the croutons, garlic, pine nuts, parsley, sage, salt, and olive oil and mix well. Stuff the game hens with this mixture and tie the legs of each one together to keep the stuffing in. Place on a spit and roast them for about 30 minutes (time will vary according to the heat of the fire and the distance of the spit from the fire). If using the oven, place the hens in a roasting pan, place in the oven, and roast for about 30 minutes. With either technique, cook the hens until their internal temperature is 160° F.

When the hens are done, remove them from the pan, cut them in half lengthwise, place them on a plate, and return them to the oven. Drain off any fat or oil from the pan, add the chicken stock and the lemon juice, and stir with a spoon. Reduce the liquid by half and serve this sauce over the hens.

YIELD: 4 servings

Faba in Frixorio
(Fried Figs and Beans with Kitchen Herbs)

This vegetarian recipe appeared in Latin in *De honesta voluptate*, a cookbook written by Platina. Da Vinci praised Platina in his notebooks and had a copy of the cookbook in his library.

INGREDIENTS

1 cup kidney beans, soaked overnight and cooked
1 cup dried figs, chopped
1 medium onion, chopped
½ teaspoon garlic, minced
½ teaspoon fresh rosemary, minced
½ teaspoon fresh basil, minced
½ teaspoon fresh thyme, minced
2 tablespoons fresh Italian parsley, finely chopped
Salt and freshly ground black pepper, to taste

In a greased skillet, combine the cooked beans with the figs and the remaining ingredients (except for the parsley) and fry, stirring often, for about 5 minutes. Serve sprinkled with the parsley.

YIELD: 4 servings

Lombartine alla Parmigiana
(Veal Cutlets with Ham and Marsala)

Leonardo wrote about hiking and collecting nature specimens near Milan and the foods that were available there. He would have enjoyed this dish before he embraced vegetarianism. Serve the veal with boiled carrots and turnips, buttered and peppered.

INGREDIENTS

4 veal cutlets, pounded lightly
2 tablespoons olive oil
¼ cup ham, chopped
2 sprigs Italian parsley, chopped
3 tablespoons grated Parmesan cheese
½ cup marsala
Salt and freshly ground black pepper

Sprinkle the cutlets on both sides with salt and pepper. Heat the butter in a skillet and brown the cutlets slowly on both sides until they are golden. In a bowl, mix together the ham, parsley, and cheese. Spread this mixture over the cutlets and pour in the marsala. Cover the skillet and cook until the steam from the marsala has melted the cheese, about 2 minutes.

YIELD: 4 servings

Fritelle da Papa Magnifici
(Superb Fritters for the Pope)

Fritters, often fried in lard, were popular during the Renaissance as both side dishes and desserts, and they contained everything from apples to anchovies. And they still taste great today, as this modern version based on a recipe in *Libro per cuoco* proves.

INGREDIENTS

> 1 cup ricotta cheese
> 2 egg whites
> 2 tablespoons flour
> 2 tablespoons pine nuts
> Vegetable oil for frying
> Confectioners' sugar

In a bowl, combine the ricotta and the egg whites and beat together until smooth. Add the flour and the pine nuts and mix well.

Heat the oil about an inch deep in a skillet until hot. Add the batter a teaspoon at a time and fry, turning once. They should be browned on both sides, but they do cook quickly. Serve immediately dusted with the sugar.

YIELD: 2 to 4 servings

Chapter Five

DA VINCI'S KITCHEN

It is ironic that Leonardo lived at the Sforza court amidst all its grandeur when he basically led a very simple life devoid of the spectacular dishes that were being served at the banquets. By examining his notebooks, we can get an inside look at the food that was part of his daily life and which differed greatly from the extravagances displayed in chapter six.

THE FRACTURED NOTEBOOKS

Beginning at about the age of thirty-seven and until his death at the age of sixty-seven, Leonardo made notes, accompanied by drawings, on a variety of subjects. These "notebooks" were mostly random, though in a few places he indicated a desire to organize them. "This is to be a collection without order, taken from many papers," he wrote on the front sheet of a manuscript about physics, "which I have copied here, hoping afterwards to arrange them according to the subjects of which they treat."

Leonardo took his notes in "mirror writing." The biographer Charles Nicholl notes: "It is correctly mirror-script, rather than just writing backwards. Not only does the whole line of script move from right to left, but each letter is formed in reverse; for instance, a Leonardo *d* looks like a *b*." Nicholl points out that there is a "strong psychological element of secrecy" in the mirror writing, not exactly a code but a way to keep his thoughts private. Of course, this secrecy did not extend to his drawings.

When Leonardo died in 1519 in France, he left all of his manuscripts and drawings to his favorite student Francesco Melzi. It is estimated that Leonardo left between fifty and 120 complete notebooks to Melzi, but today only twenty-eight (some say twenty-seven) survive in various versions. This is because after Melzi died in 1570, Leonardo was mostly forgotten, and the value of his notes and drawings was not recognized. And of course, the mirror writing was difficult to decipher. Melzi's heirs gave away or sold many of the notebooks, and they were dispersed across Europe. Many other people had access to Leonardo's work, often making their own notes on top of his.

Scholars disagree about how many pages of Leonardo's notebooks survive today, with estimates varying between 5,000 and 7,000 pages. This discrepancy probably exists because of the vague definition of what precisely constitutes a page. Scholars estimate that is about half of Leonardo's total output, which is estimated at 13,000 pages.

LEONARDO'S PRESCRIPTION FOR LIFE

Written as a poem in 1515, four years before his death and when he was ill in Rome, this is Leonardo's guide for living:

If you want to be healthy observe this regime.
Do not eat when you have no appetite, and dine lightly,
Chew well, and whatever you take into you
Should be well-cooked and of simple ingredients.
He who takes medicine is ill advised.
Beware anger and avoid stuffy air.
Stay standing a while when you get up from a meal.
Make sure you do not sleep at midday.
Let your wine be mixed with water, take little at a time
Not between meals, nor on an empty stomach.
Neither delay nor prolong your visit to the toilet.
If you take exercise, let it not be too strenuous.
Do not lie with your stomach upward and your head
Downward. Be well covered at night,
And rest your head and keep your mind cheerful.
Avoid wantonness and keep to this diet.

In the late sixteenth century, scholars began the process of literally cutting and pasting all the manuscripts into codices, which have been given names such as the *Codex Atlanticus*, which has nothing to do with the ocean, but rather is so named because it was atlas-sized. Specifically, it was originally a huge leather-bound volume about two feet tall when it was assembled by the bibliophile Pompeo Leoni. In the 1960s, the *Codex Atlanticus* was dismantled, reordered, and made into twelve leather-bound volumes that now reside at the Biblioteca Ambrosiana in Milan.

The *Codex Atlanticus* is the most important of all the codices and contains studies of mathematics, geometry, botany, zoology, and hydraulics, as well as notes on theoretical and practical aspects of painting. Also included are sketches of war machines, working machines, flying machines, boats, and architectural studies.

The notebooks and the codices made from them are a confusing mass of information. Michael White comments that "Leonardo's originals have been as mutilated as the corpses over which he often labored. Pages were torn from bound books and dispersed, damaged, and in some cases lost completely, and this has disrupted further efforts to follow the flow of his thought and the progression of his ideas." Serge Bramly wrote of the thousands of pages in the codices: "This immense jigsaw puzzle has not yet yielded up all its secrets."

LEONARDO'S LARDER

It wasn't only work for Leonardo in Milan. He occasionally went on hikes in the mountains, and he appreciated the Valtellina region northeast of Lake Como. Leonardo commented on the food and wine there, writing in his notebooks that "they make a strong wine there, in good quantities, but there are so many cattle that the locals will tell you they make more milk than wine." He went on to comment about how inexpensive the food was compared to the food in Milan: "The wine costs no more than one soldo a bottle, and a pound of veal one soldo, and salt ten denari, and butter the same, and you can get a basketful of eggs for one soldo." It is enlightening to know that a basket of eggs was equivalent to a pound of veal and a bottle of wine, because we have little documentary evidence of what the various foodstuffs sold for. And in the country, Leonardo said that the portions of food served at the inns were larger. "The pound up here has thirty ounces," he wrote.

In contrast to the elaborate court feasts, from what we can glean from Leonardo's shopping lists in his notebooks, the fare he was serving himself and his assistants appears to be relatively ordinary. Conspicuously missing from these lists, which were undoubtedly not comprehensive, were poultry, fish, veal, squash, cheese, lard, olive oil, pasta (unless he made his own), root and tuber crops of any kind, and pitted fruits like peaches, apples, and rice.

ODE TO WINE, BY ANGELO POLIZIANO

Bacchus, Bacchus, shout with glee,
Keep on stowing wine inside;
Then we'll wreck this place noisily.
Drink up, you, and get pie-eyed.
Can't dance any more, I'm fried.
Everybody cry hail, hurray!

—from "Orfeo: Sacrifice of the Bacchantes in Honor of the Bacchus."
Poliziano, who did not believe in wine moderation, was a tutor
to the sons of Lorenzo de' Medici in the fifteenth century.

Since Leonardo had a copy of Platina's book, we have a window into early Renaissance food beliefs. As it turns out, Platina wrote about nearly every food item in Leonardo's pantry. Note that very little of this material is from Martino, some of it is from Pliny the Elder, and Platina consulted many other sources, including Avicenna, Pythagoras, Apuleius, Columella, Celsus, Martial, and Virgil.

In the description of Leonardo's larder that follows, I have placed the food items that he mentioned in bold type. In lieu of Leonardo's words on his own food, also included are Platina's observations on Leonardo's food purchases, because they may have influenced Leonardo, who praised Platina, especially for his coverage of simple, or vegetarian, foods. We don't know, of course, if Leonardo believed everything that Platina wrote, but there were no other food or recipe books in Leonardo's library, so it's a good guess that he did. In some cases I have added additional material from Martino to illustrate how some of the larder ingredients were prepared in the early Renaissance.

DAIRY

There are only two items in this category. **Buttermilk**, the liquid left after butter was churned, was used in baking. It is interesting that **eggs** would be on the list, as the Sforza complex undoubtedly kept chickens. Maestro Martino has fourteen egg recipes, including Eggs Cooked in the Ashes, Eggs on a Spit, Stuffed Fried Eggs, and Eggs Disguised as Ravioli:

Make some pastry as you would for *lasagne*, but not too thin
and not too soft. Break over it some fresh eggs, sprinkling
each one with sugar, sweet spices, and a little salt, and enclose
each one in the pastry as you would ravioli. Boil or fry them,
though they are best fried. You can make them like turnovers,
using the same ingredients but adding a little verjuice if you
wish, baking them as you would tarts, or frying them. But
don't let the eggs overcook, as the more you cook them the
harder they become, and the worse they are.

Although Platina does not mention **buttermilk** specifically, he does
have a short treatise on milk in general. He writes that goat's milk is the
best, then sheep's milk, with cow's milk coming in third. "One must, however, avoid too much use of milk," he writes, "for it makes the keenness
of the eyes duller and generates stones in kidneys and bladder." Of **eggs**,
Platina insists that the most healthful are those fertilized by the rooster,
and the most flavorful are those laid by a fat hen rather than a lean one.
Eggs are a cure for "cough, sore windpipes, a hoarse voice, and those spitting blood."

PLATINA'S SCRAMBLED EGGS

With a paddle or spoon, mix with ground cheese eggs which have cracked
and well beaten with a bit of water or milk. When these are mixed, cook in
butter or oil. They will be more pleasant if cooked only a little and never
turned while cooking. If you want the color of herbs in them, add chard,
parsley, some borage juice, mint, marjoram, and a little sage.

FRUIT

The word "fruit" is used in a generic sense, which may have meant buy any
fruit available at market. **Melon** is listed, which is slightly ironic because
according to classical medicine, melons should only be eaten at the beginning of a meal, on an empty stomach, accompanied by some decent wine.
Pope Paul II was thought to have died from eating ice-cold melons in the
summer, but since melons were the pope's favorite food, Martino included
a melon soup in his cookbook. The historian Bruno Laurioux observes:
"As a worthy servant of Paul II, he could hardly leave out the recipe for a
Menestra di melloni which may even have precipitated his master's sudden

death, attributed by contemporaries to acute indigestion after eating the melons to which he was addicted."

Platina writes that a **melon**, when served with the rind and seeds removed, "soothes the stomach and gently softens the bowels." Because of its "dampness," a melon is harmful to the nerves, but this effect can be lessened by drinking a glass of wine "because it is a sort of antidote against the coldness and stiffness of the melon." Platina notes that "[t]he emperor Albinus, however, was so delighted with this fruit that he ate 100 Campanian peaches and ten melons from Ostia at one meal."

Grapes were on the list, and according to Sir Robert Dallington, who visited Italy in 1596, the best grapes to eat were *Moscatello* and *Rimadlesca*. "Well-matured" grapes "are less unhealthy than other fruits which are eaten raw," Platina advises, "and eaten as a first course, they cause almost no harm." Grape seeds should not be eaten because "they are too difficult to digest and too harmful to nutrition." Platina also preferred the wine from white grapes because it is sweeter. To Dallington, **mulberries** were "another of the greatest commodities of Tuscany" he would "not forget." Martino has a nice relish made from them, Mulberry Relish, presumably a spread for bread or rolls:

> Take some peeled almonds and pound well with a few white breadcrumbs, stir in the mulberries, but do not bash or pound them, to avoid crushing the little seeds inside. Then add some cinnamon, ginger, and a little nutmeg and pass everything through a sieve.

Mulberries move the bowels and urine very quickly but they "provide little nourishment." Platina notes for the record, "In Egypt and Cyprus [the mulberry tree] produces fruit with most abundant juice which has three colors: first it is white, then red, and finally it is very dark, as if it were sprinkled with the blood of the Egyptian maiden Thisbe."

FUNGI

Fungi mushrooms were often cooked with garlic and a silver coin. If the coin turned black, legend goes, the mushroom was poisonous. Also, they were cleaned very well and grilled over the fire or boiled in water and then fried in olive oil or lard.

"**Mushrooms** are also eaten but have led to crime in many cases," Platina asserts. He knew that there were good mushrooms and poisonous ones. "I would want mushrooms picked by those experienced with the regions," he

Da Vinci's blackberries
Sunbelt Archives

notes, "and even they are deceived, for we know that certain households have died in our era." He advises that some people cook mushrooms with garlic to counteract the poison, and he is not a fungus fan: "Cooked any way you want, even though they satisfy the palate, they are considered the very worst, for they are difficult to digest and generate destructive humors."

ON TRUFFLES, BY PLATINA

This food is nourishing, as pleases Galen, and indeed very much so, and arouses passion. Hence it is that the aphrodisiac tables of voluptuaries and nobles often use it that they may be more ready for passion. If that is done for fertility, it is praiseworthy, but if it is done for libidinous behavior, as many idle and immoderate people are accustomed to, it is entirely detestable.

Grains

We have something of a culinary mystery here, as **corn** is mentioned three times in the notebooks. "Have some ears of corn of large size sent from Florence," Leonardo wrote, abbreviating "grano" as "gra." Also, there are references to **white maize** and **red maize**, using the word *melica*. Although translated as "maize," the Latin word *melica* refers to a grass with a sweet sap (*mel* means "honey") and is thought to be sorghum. It is used to make such foods as couscous, sorghum flour, porridge, and molasses. Most experts believe that corn spread rapidly throughout Italy in the early sixteenth century, and according to Leonardo, it had reached northern Italy.

In a 1975 article, "Pre-Columbian Maize in the Old World," M. D. W. Jeffreys theorizes that somehow maize was already in the Mediterranean before Columbus, because it is unlikely that if it had been introduced into Spain in 1493, it could be documented growing in the East Indies by 1496. See the complete discussion of this mystery in chapter seven.

Bran or **meal** is the outer layer of grains like wheat and oats; it was added to water and used to take the salt out of salted fish being cooked in it. **Wheat** is mentioned several times, and since Leonardo was buying **bread**, which was made with soft wheat, the wheat he was buying was probably hard wheat, used to make macaroni. Clifford Wright notes that hard wheat is high in gluten and low in moisture content, and "[t]hese characteristics of hard wheat are important because, first, it prevents the stretching and breaking of pasta during the curing and drying process and, second, because it maintains its texture and taste better during the cooking process than does soft wheat."

Flour is listed, too, and it was probably soft wheat flour for baking bread, rolls, or pies. **Millet**, which we think of as bird food, was essentially a peasant food, boiled in a meat broth to make a gruel. Millet makes "porridge and very sweet bread," writes Platina. "The principle use of millet kneaded with must is for leaven, since it lasts a year." He also noted that "[m]illet and Italian millet deplete the earth and for this reason should not be sown among vines or fruit trees."

There is no mention of **corn, white maize, red maize,** or **bran** in Platina's book, but he does discuss **wheat**, which is "easily digested, purges, and cools. Its frequent use closes the fibers of the liver and spleen," and "nothing is more productive and pleasant than wheat, which nourishes much more if it is grown in the hills and not on the plain," Platina states. The

bread made from the wheat flour is leavened, sourdough-style, but "[l]et the baker be careful not to put in too much or too little leaven, for, from the former, bread can acquire a sour taste, and, from the latter, it can become too heavy to digest and too unhealthy, since it binds the bowels."

Herbs and Spices

The word "herbs" was used in a generic sense, again probably meaning whatever was available. Not only seasonings, **mint** and **parsley** were primary ingredients in Martino's Herb Soup. **Thyme** was used to season chicken, and Martino uses it in a green sauce.

Nutmeg was prominent in relishes, and **mustard**—probably the most popular condiment of the era—was used on meats and in egg dishes. An example is Martino's Mustard Relish, called Red, or Purple, Mustard:

> Take your mustard seeds and pound them well, then take raisins and pound as well as you possibly can. Add a little toasted bread, some sandalwood and cinnamon, and a bit of verjuice, vinegar, or grape must to thin the mixture a little, then pass it through a sieve.

Buckwheat is commonly thought to be a grain, but it's actually the seed of an herb. The seeds are used to make buckwheat flour; buckwheat groats are hulled, and the crushed seeds are cooked like rice. Buckwheat groats are "among the grains of good juice" and are a "bread-maker that makes a good broth," notes Platina. **Pepper**, which is not mentioned in the notebooks but was certainly used by Leonardo, was thought to grow on trees, an idea borrowed from Pliny. "Pepper is warm and dry, and for this reason it warms the stomach and liver, is harmful to the bilious, releases and drives wind from the bowels and moves the urine."

Mint "makes the heart glad, helps the stomach, kills worms, and is especially effective against the bite of a rabid dog," writes Platina, while **parsley** roots "act wonderfully against poison," and because bitter, the parsley root "suits medicine more than eating." Wild **thyme** "is effective against snakes, and when it is cooked in vinegar and smeared on the temples, it takes away headaches wonderfully." Cultivated thyme, "when taken in food, dispels dim eyesight, kills worms, moves the urine, brings on the menstrual period in women, and draws out stillbirths." **Nutmeg** "helps the human body by its force and fragrance, sharpens weakened vision of the eyes, settles vomit, and induces appetite by soothing the stomach and liver." **Mustard**, like many of the herbs and spices described by Platina, is as much of a medicine as a food. "When smeared on an ailment of the body, it shows the force of its burning," Platina writes, indicating the early use of a mustard plaster. It also "drives out ills in the lungs, lightens a chronic cough, makes spitting easy...warms the stomach and liver...creates thirst, and stimulates passion."

LEGUMES

Beans, undoubtedly fava beans, are used in several of Martino's recipes, but **kidney beans**, on Leonardo's shopping list, are not mentioned by Martino. Since kidney beans, *Phaseolus vulgaris*, are a New World variety, they would not have been known by Martino, and it seems unlikely that they would have been in Italy so soon after 1492. Leonardo used the term "fagiuoli" to describe them, but fava beans are simply *fave* in modern Italian. Interestingly, *fagioli* is Italian for New World beans. **Peas** do show up in in a recipe Martino calls Fresh Peas with Salt Meat. After giving some advice on how to plant the pea, Platina notes that "it is sweet and less flatulent and harmful than the broad bean."

Platina calls the fava **bean** the "broad bean," and it appears in several recipes. According to him:

> Pythagoras abstained from eating broad bean porridge: either because, as he himself used to say, the souls of the dead reside in them, or else because this food, by its inflation, is uncommonly contrary to those seeking peace of mind, and it arouses the passion that resides in the testicles, which they used to say were similar to beans.

Platina, like Leonardo, mentions the mysterious **kidney bean** and even calls it "phaseolus," which is the genus name for many New World beans today. Platina is not kind to the kidney beans, writing that they "fill the head with gross and bad humors and bring on dreams, and indeed bad ones." He also writes that they are fattening but they do "lubricate the bowels." After eating kidney beans, "it is very necessary to drink pure wine."

> **FAVE**
>
> "The fava bean has had the worst reputation of any of the common foods, and the most peculiar history. Pisanelli maintained that the bean would provoke *horribili sospiri*—horrible sighs. The gentle and tolerant Castelvetro said it could only be eaten by pregnant women, unwise children, pigs, and other animals. Other Renaissance writers believed that it induced nightmares and corrupt dreams. And although Tanara described the fresh bean as "food for princes," it is usually associated with the plebs, and poverty. The association was not unreasonable; the fava was one of the fundamental foods of the countryside."
>
> —Berengario delle Cinqueterre

MEAT

The word "meat" is used, but the type of meat to buy is unspecified. **Beef** and **good beef**, *bon bove*, are mentioned and were the main ingredients in stews, meatballs, turnovers, and kebabs. Platina both praises and denigrates beef and good beef. In the first place:

> No one doubts that beef, the label under which I list bull, cow and veal, is of great use to people by intelligence, drawing vehicles, milk, cheese, and hide for use in shoes. Hence it was a fact that among the ancients one was considered as guilty of capital offense to kill an ox without cause as one who killed a man.

But, don't eat beef, because it is "very hard to both cook and to digest" and offers "gross, disturbed, and melancholic nourishment," says Platina. Additionally, "it drives a person toward quartan fever, eczema, and scaly skin disease." It is possible that these negative comments about beef influenced Leonardo, who in his later years embraced vegetarianism.

SWEETS

The only sweet mentioned besides **sugar** was **anise** candy. Leonardo mentions in his notebooks that his assistant Salai stole some money to buy anise sweets. Platina liked anise, writing that it improves the appetite and "represses the vapors that are seeking the head." It eliminates bad breath, "moves the urine, cures headaches, is good for the nerves, and increases passion."

Vegetables

The word "vegetables" is used in a generic sense, as is **salad**. I presume "salad" is a generic term for salad ingredients like lettuce and carrots rather than a salad mix like the ones sold in today's supermarkets. Martino doesn't mention them, but they were used between courses as a palate refresher in court dinners.

Platina describes the ingredients in a seasoned **salad** as "lettuce, borage, mint, calamint, fennel, parsley, wild thyme, marjoram, chervil, sow-thistle, lancet, nightshade, flower of fennel, and several other aromatic herbs." They are washed, drained, salted, and then sprinkled with oil and vinegar.

Miscellaneous

Vinegar was used with olive oil in salads, and, as Gillian Riley notes: "It had many uses in cooking, salads, pickled and preserved food, and as a refreshing drink, diluted with water and sometimes mixed with honey; it also had many medicinal uses." Vinegar, warns Platina, "is quite damaging, although it is given to melancholics, those with inflamed eyes, those laboring under pain in the joints, paralytics, or those subject to spasms, because it makes its way, with the bad humors, to the nerves and joints." He advises moderation and pouring vinegar over the bites of poisonous animals and notes that M. Agrippa "was freed from the worst pain of gout in his last years by soaking his feet in warm vinegar."

Sugar was the sweetener of candies, cookies, and pies and was used to create elaborate sculptures for feasts. The whiter the sugar the better, Platina advises. The "ancients used sugar merely for medicinal purposes," but by Leonardo's time that usage was expanded and sugar was an ingredient in many of the dishes in both Martino's and Platina's books. By melting sugar, writes Platina, "we make almonds...pine nuts, hazelnuts, coriander, anise, cinnamon, and many other things into sweets."

Wine was the drink of choice in Leonardo's house, and consumption of wine in northern Italy was about eight-tenths of a liter per person per day. The best drinking wines, according to Sir Robert Dallington, were *Passerina* and *Lugliola*. Platina praises wine but urges moderation and diluting the wine. Then he describes the various wines produced not only in Italy, but also in Corsica and Greece, and ends his commentary with the observation that his time "produces better wines than men."

ON WINE, BY PLATINA

Hence it is that nothing aids tired bodies more swiftly, if it is used moderately. In a similar manner, nothing is more harmful if moderation is absent. Because of drunkenness, men become trembling, troublesome, pallid, befouled, forgetful, bleary-eyed, sterile, slow to procreate, gray haired, and old before their time. It is enough for us briefly to enumerate what wines are valuable, but first I urge the readers not to think on this account that I am very greedy for wine, since no one drinks it more diluted than I, by custom and by nature.

LEONARDO'S KITCHEN DESIGNS AND INVENTIONS

In 1482, at the age of thirty, Leonardo moved from Florence and joined the court of Ludovico Sforza, the duke of Milan. In addition to creating masterworks like *The Last Supper*, Leonardo was a musician, a designer of war machines and defenses, and a producer of elaborate court spectacles like the "Feast of Paradise." In one instance, he was even doing some remodeling of the Sforza castle, most probably the apartments of Duchess Beatrice. So while working on *The Last Supper*, he was supervising remodeling of his lord's castle and also taking on some outside design work, probably on the mansion of Mariolo de' Guiscardi, an important Milanese courtier. In the *Codex Atlanticus*, Leonardo gives his ideas on kitchen design:

> The large room for the retainers should be away from the
> kitchen, so the master of the house may not hear their clatter.
> And let the kitchen be convenient for washing the pewter so
> it may not be seen being carried through the house.... The
> larder, woodstore, kitchen, chicken-coop, and servants' hall
> should be adjoining, for convenience. And the garden, stable,
> and manure-heaps should also be adjoining.... Food from
> the kitchen may be served through wide, low windows, or
> on tables that turn on swivels.... The window of the kitchen
> should be in front of the buttery [pantry] so firewood can be
> taken in.

A Renaissance garden, c. 1500
North Wind Picture Archives

Unfortunately, any drawings Leonardo might have made of kitchens have never been found. But from other passages in his notebooks, we can get an idea of what foods he appreciated and what he was buying.

Always the inventor, Leonardo was interested in saving human effort. In drawings in the *Codex Atlanticus*, he invented two devices for turning meat on a spit over the fire to save effort on the part of the cooks. One of them used a counterweight lowered by rope wrapped around a cylinder. As the weight was lowered, it turned the cylinder, which turned the gears that turned the two spits. Of course, this invention required that the cooks turn the cylinder to hoist the counterweight once it had reached the ground.

The second automatic spit-turner is more ingenious because it harnessed the power of heated air. It is the first appearance in history of an air screw. Bern Dibner, writing in *The Unknown Leonardo*, notes: "Like an ingenious home handyman, he put his discovery to practical use in the kitchen...it promised to liberate the cook." Rising heated air in a chimney turned the vaned turbine, which turned the gears and the spit placed over the fire. "The roast will turn slow or fast depending on whether the fire is small or strong," notes Leonardo.

Devices like this were actually used in Renaissance kitchens. Italian food experts Capatti and Montanari explain: "A more advanced type of skewer involved a fan that, when set in motion by the hot air rising above the flames, caused a cylindrical cogwheel to rotate; this in turn moved the serrated wheel attached to the rod." It is tempting to believe that Leonardo provided the inspiration for this type of spit-turner, but that will probably never be known because we have no information on whether or not he showed his notebook designs to anyone. Leonardo is believed to have been very secretive about his notebooks, and they were never published during the Renaissance.

But we do know the primary result of the evolution of semi-automated spit-turners. In Scappi's *Opera* there is an illustration of Scappi's own device that winds up like a clock by way of the large drum at the bottom. When released, the chain turns the wheels and cogs that rotate the three spits on which the meats are skewered. Each spit turns at a different rate and is a different distance from the heat, giving the cook great leeway to cook different roasts at the same time. In the illustration, the top spit has a leg of lamb or veal that needs a longer cooking time than the sausages and small birds on the bottom spit. This style of spit-turner became common in Europe in later centuries, and some examples that have survived

Model of Leonardo's alchemic stove
Museo Ideale Leonardo da Vinci; photo by Marco Budinis

the centuries still function, although they need an engineer to maintain and adjust them.

Leonardo's attempt to control and better utilize the cooking fire was further refined in what some sources believe is the first working barbecue unit. The wood was placed in the bottom of the unit through an opening that also served as the vent for air to enter and keep the fire going. The food to be grilled was placed on a grate on top of the unit. The device is remarkably similar to barbecue units produced today.

Like with most of Leonardo's inventions, it is not known if any of these devices were actually constructed. Leonardo himself was never satisfied with his inventions. In the words of Bern Dibner, "No solution was ever adequate, for he would return later to some similar device to accomplish the same task by using different parts or a different assembly of parts."

Other, non-food-related inventions included his "tank," a device that resembles a flying saucer with guns protruding that was able to roll along the ground, giant automatic crossbows, large mortars firing shrapnel shells, flying machines, diving devices, and even more mundane devices like mechanical looms.

Biographer of Leonardo, Michael White, observes:

> The most distinctive aspect of his work as a military designer, and indeed an obsession which showed itself in many of Leonardo's ideas and plans, was his devotion to the notion of automation. This is particularly startling when we recall the world in which he lived, a civilization in which the fastest speeds were attained on horseback, in which carts and carriages provided the most sophisticated means of transport, a time three centuries before the first steam engine.

An interesting debate has evolved over another of Leonardo's inventions, the lock that made canals navigable. The Milanese cleric, Giovanni Ambrogio Mazenta (1565–1635), had thirteen of Leonardo's manuscripts in his possession and wrote in his memoirs about Leonardo's technical achievements, which many later scholars have insisted were never built. Ladislao Reti, in his essay "Elements of Machines," writes: "The information contained is significant because it is based on the widespread tradition still alive at the time" about the practical uses of Leonardo's ideas. "Mazenta writes of 'Leonardo's invention of machines and gates to level, intercommunicate and make navigable' the waterways connecting the Lombard lakes." He also mentions "many machines depicted in [Leonardo's] books, that have been put to use in the region of Milan, like weirs, locks, and gates, mostly invented by Leonardo."

Is this just hyperbole based on Leonardo's enormous reputation as an inventor? And what does it have to do with food? Well, as with many things about Leonardo, we don't know for certain. But the legend lives on. In his 1971 book, *The Food of Italy*, Waverly Root observes: "When Leonardo da Vinci's invention of the lock made the Po navigable and extended the reach of the Naviglio, it brought into Milan rich cargoes of cream, butter, *mascarpone* cheese, honey, vegetables, and fruit."

Leaving Milan

We have seen that Leonardo was busy with many projects, and even when he was at a party he was working. Giovanni Paolo Lomazzo (1538–1600), a painter who became a writer, collected anecdotes about Leonardo like this one:

> There is a story told by men of his time, who were his servants, that he once wished to make a picture of some laughing peasants (though in the event he did not paint it, but only did a drawing). He picked out certain men whom he thought fitted the bill, and having become acquainted with them, he arranged a party for them, with the help of some friends, and sitting down opposite them, he started to tell them the craziest and most ridiculous things in the world, in such a way that he made them fall about laughing. And so without them knowing he observed all their gestures and their reactions to his ridiculous talk, and impressed them on his mind, and after they left he retired to his room, and there made a perfect drawing which moved people to laughter when they looked at it, just as much as if they were listening to Leonardo's stories at the party.

We can speculate that quite a bit of that wine on Leonardo's shopping list was served at this party. The images referred to by Lomazzo are known as Leonardo's "grotesques," or as Leonardo called them, the "buffoonish, ridiculous and really pitiable."

During this time in the early 1490s, Leonardo was making progress on the bronze horse, the monument for Ludovico's father. For the wedding and feast of Ludivico's niece Bianca to the Holy Roman Emperor, Maximilian of Habsburg, in November of 1493, Leonardo presented the clay model of the bronze horse of Ludovico's father to the delight of the people of Milan. Giorgio Vasari wrote of it: "Those who saw the great clay model that Leonardo made considered that they had never seen a finer or more magnificent piece of work." Leonardo took careful notes on the casting of the horse in bronze, but that would never happen. Worried about the possibility of a French invasion of his territory, Ludovico sent the tons of bronze that would have been used for the horse to his father-in-law, Ercole

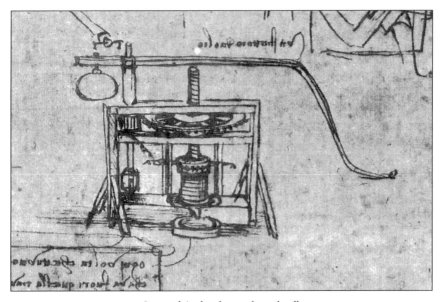

Leonardo's plan for an olive oil mill
Museo Ideale Leonardo da Vinci; photo by Marco Budinis

d'Este, who used it to make cannons in 1494. Ludovico was in debt to d'Este—he owed him 3,000 ducats—so perhaps the bronze was a partial repayment. "A tremendous blow to Leonardo and his studio" is how the biographer Nicholl describes the transfer of the bronze, but Leonardo only writes, "Of the horse I will say nothing because I know the times."

Leonardo apparently understood the situation, and, besides, he soon had another project, a painting for Ludovico at the refectory of the Dominican monastery of Santa Maria delle Grazie: the wall mural known as *The Last Supper*. Leonardo was faced with an interesting challenge while painting *The Last Supper*. At the supper table, as portrayed in his quasi-fresco, how would the disciples react after Jesus says, "Verily I say unto you, that one of you shall betray me"? In his notebooks, Leonardo plans how he will paint their reactions:

> One who was drinking and has left the glass in its position and turned his head towards the speaker.... Another who has turned, holding a knife in his hand, knocks over a glass on the table.... Another leans forward to see the speaker, shading his eyes with his hand.

In the painting, the figure of Judas even spills a salt cellar. Some of the disciples pictured are real portraits of Milanese courtiers and popular citizens. Leonardo paints them in a manner different from the versions of the supper that preceded his—instead of a linear grouping along the table, Leonardo goes for a wave perspective, as Nicholl puts it, "formed of four subgroups, each of three disciples: knots and huddles of men suddenly in crisis. Leonardo has found his dramatic moment. . . ." And that moment comes during the most famous supper in world history.

While he was working on *The Last Supper*, Leonardo was having financial problems—specifically problems with collecting his salary from Ludovico. In his notebooks, he drafted a letter to the duke: "It vexes me greatly that you should have found me in need and . . . that having to earn my living has forced me to interrupt the work and to attend to lesser matters. . . ." The "lesser matters" were probably the remodeling and painting work he was doing for the duchess.

In reality, the ongoing war had drained Ludovico's resources. His wife died in 1497 in childbirth, and the French were now allied with Florence and Naples against Milan. There was an uprising against Ludovico led by Gian Giacomo Trivulzio in August of 1499, and days afterward, Ludovico fled to Austria. The French triumphantly entered Milan in October, and one of their first actions, after burning, looting, and raping, was to have the archers use Leonardo's famous clay horse, the model for the statue, for target practice, nearly destroying it.

Leonardo got the message, transferred his savings to a Florentine bank, and fled Milan in December of 1499. "It was a different Leonardo who leaves now," writes Nicholl, "forty-seven years old, his chamois jerkin buttoned up against the cold, quitting the uncertain accomplishments of the Sforza years for an even more uncertain future." And the historian J. H. Plumb observes of the Sforzas, "The great horse designed by Leonardo for Ludovico in memory of his father seems curiously symbolic of their destiny—conceived in grandeur, executed in clay, never cast, ruined by the French, and destroyed by time."

Prophecies and Fables

Before he left Milan the first time, Leonardo wrote, probably as entertainment for the court, a series of "prophecies" in the form of riddles, and some of them concern food: "There will be many who will flay their mother and turn her skin inside out." (Farmers who till the land.) And he

Model of Leonardo's olive oil mill
Museo Ideale Leonardo da Vinci; photo by Marco Budinis

Model of Leonardo's water-powered wheat mill along the Po River
Museo Nazionale della Scienza e della Tecnologia

writes ironically, "The nut-tree by the roadside showed off to travelers the richness of its fruits; everyone stoned it."

"With merciless blows many little children will be taken from the arms of their mothers and thrown to the ground and then torn to pieces." (Fruits, walnuts, olives.) Nature is seen as being exploited by man—harvest is an act of wounding. However, olives are seen in another way: "And things will descend with fury from above, and will give us nourishment and light."

"Men will severely beat what gives them life." (Those who thresh grain.)

"Innocent children shall be taken from their nurses and will die with great wounds at the hands of cruel men. (Baby goats.)

"And many will be robbed of their stores and their food, and will be cruelly submerged and drowned by folks devoid of reason." (Bees.)

The biographer Kenneth Clark writes that these "prophecies" are not jokes. Given Leonardo's love of animals, they "represent his refusal to take as a matter of course the suffering which man's technical skill has allowed him to inflict on the other animals." Another biographer, Serge Bramly, believes that these prophecies "that turn on the identification of children may reflect wounds suffered from illegitimacy and his parents' separation." Leonardo's sentiment toward animals seems unusual in light of the fact that he designed machines so that men could kill each other more easily, but then Leonardo tends to be enigmatic.

Leonardo also lamented: "Eggs which being eaten cannot produce chickens. Oh, how many will those be who will never be born?" On the other hand, of course, Leonardo had eggs on his shopping list. This ambivalence surfaced again, when Leonardo wrote his legend "The Wine and Mohammed," even though wine, too, was on his shopping list.

> Wine, the divine juice of the grape, finding itself in a golden and richly wrought cup on Mohammed's table, was puffed up with pride at so much honor; when it was struck by a contrary mood, saying to itself: "What am I about, that I rejoice, not perceiving that I am now nearing my death and that I shall leave my golden abode in this cup in order to enter the foul and fetid caverns of the human body and be transmuted from a fragrant and delicious liquor into a foul and base fluid. And, as though so much evil were not enough, I for a long time have to lie in hideous receptacles, together with other fetid and corrupt matter cast out from human intestines." And it

cried to heaven imploring vengeance for so much damage,
and that an end be henceforth put to so much insult, and
since this country produced the finest and best grapes in the
whole world, these at least should not be made into wine.
Then Jove caused the wine drunk by Mohammed to rise in
spirit to his brain, contaminating it and making him mad, and
giving birth to so many follies that when he had recovered, he
made a law that no Asiatic should drink wine; and henceforth
the vine was left free with its fruit.

As soon as wine enters the stomach, it begins to ferment
and swell; then the spirit of that man begins to abandon his
body, rising toward heaven, and the brain finds itself parting
from the body. Then it begins to degrade him, and makes him
rave like a madman, and then he commits irreparable errors,
killing his friends.

Leonardo tends to exaggerate a bit; but this is a legend, after all, and
it is entirely possible that he is writing this tongue-in-cheek. Not only
is wine on his shopping lists, Leonardo admits to buying it. In 1495, he
wrote: "On Tuesday I bought wine for the morning, on Friday the 4th day
of September the same." So not only is Leonardo buying wine, he's drinking it in the morning! Bramly writes, without specific attribution, that
Leonardo advised: "Wine is good, but at table, water is preferable."

In Leonardo's fables, contained within his notebooks, trees, plants, animals, and even rocks become sentient creatures, and he presents a picture
of the Italian countryside. In his fable "The Chestnut and the Fig Tree,"
Leonardo again addresses the idea that harvesting fruits and nuts from
trees is cruel:

The chestnut, seeing a man upon the fig-tree, bending the
boughs toward him and plucking the ripe fruit which he put
into his open mouth to destroy and gnaw with his hard teeth,
tossed its long boughs and with tumultuous rustle exclaimed:
"O fig! How much less are you protected by nature than I.
See how with me my sweet offspring are set in close array:
first clothed in soft wrappers over which is the hard but softly
lined husk; and not content with taking this care of me, and
giving them so strong a shelter, she has placed over this sharp
and close-set spines so that the hand of man cannot hurt me."
Then the fig-tree and its offspring began to laugh and after the
laughter it said: "You know man to be of such ingenuity that

he will bereave you of your fruits by means of rods and stones
and stakes; and when they are fallen, he will trample them
with his feet or hit them with stones so that your offspring
will emerge from their armor crushed and maimed; while I am
touched carefully by his hands and not like you with sticks
and stones."

The point of the fable is that egotistical people who look down on others are put in their place, but the irony here is that no matter how well protected the "offspring" are, they both end up in the stomach of man.

In another fable about trees, Leonardo seems to be justifying his own lack of procreation:

> The fig-tree standing by the side of the elm and seeing that
> its boughs were without fruit and that it nevertheless had the
> audacity to keep the sun from its own unripe figs said reprov-
> ingly: "O elm, are you not ashamed to stand in front of me?
> But wait till my offspring are ripe and you will see where you
> are!" But when her fruit were ripe, a troop of soldiers pass-
> ing by fell upon the fig-tree and tore off the figs, cutting and
> breaking the boughs. And as the fig-tree stood thus maimed
> in all its limbs, the elm-tree asked it: "O fig-tree, how much
> better it is to be without offspring than to be brought through
> them into so miserable a plight."

In the fable "The Privet and the Blackbird," Leonardo shames people who think that the world revolves around them, again using the theme of the taking of fruit from the plant:

> The privet feeling its tender boughs, loaded with young fruit,
> pricked by the sharp claws and beak of the insolent black-
> bird, complained to the blackbird with piteous remonstrance
> entreating it that since it stole the delicious fruits it should at
> least spare the leaves which served to protect them from the
> burning rays of the sun, and desist from scratching the tender
> bark with its sharp claws. To this the blackbird replied with
> an angry upbraiding: "Oh, be silent, uncultured shrub! Do
> you not know that nature made you produce their fruits for
> my nourishment; do you not see that you are in this world to
> serve me with food; do you not know, base creature, that next
> winter you will be food and prey for the fire?" To these words

the tree listened patiently, and not without tears. Shortly afterwards the blackbird was caught in a net and boughs were cut to make a cage and imprison it. Branches were cut from the pliant privet, to serve for the plaited twigs of the cage; and seeing that it was the cause of the blackbird's loss of liberty the privet rejoicingly said: "O blackbird, I am here and not yet burnt as you have foresaid. I shall see you in prison before you see me burnt."

Leonardo was something of a fatalist in these fables: "Man and the animals are merely a passage and channel for food, a tomb for other animals, a haven for the dead, giving life by the death of others, a coffer full of corruption." He goes on morbidly to write, "Men shall come forth out of graves changed to winged creatures [flies that feed on corpses] and they shall attack other men, taking away their food even from their hands and tables."

But Leonardo went on and had some fun.

THE COMPANY OF THE CAULDRON

In the early 1500s, the Florentine sculptor Giovan Francesco Rustici formed a group called the Company of the Cauldron and staged banquets. Each member of the group could bring four guests and was expected to supply one creative dish. Waverly Root states that it was the first cooking academy since Roman times. "The result sounds like a deliberate parody of the décor and food of a grand Medici court banquet," notes Roy Strong. Paul Barolsky, author of the interesting book *Infinite Jest: Wit and Humor in Italian Renaissance Art*, describes one of the events:

> One of the most extraordinary of these was made by Andrea del Sarto, who confected an octagonal structure like the Bapistery of Florence. The pavement was made of jelly, its columns, which looked like porphyry [colorful Egyptian rock], were large sausages, the bases and capitals were made of parmesan cheese and the tribune of marzipan. Sarto's playful tour de force in what might be called gastroaesthetics (a neglected field) is reminiscent of the witty and elaborate culinary creations described by Petronius in the *Satyricon*....

The first Leonardo biographer, Giorgio Vasari, completes the description:

> In the middle was a choral music-rest made of cold veal with
> a book of lasagna that had letters and notes to sing of [made
> of] pepper grains and those who sang and read were thrushes
> cooked with open mouths and held up by certain cassock-
> like clothing made of thin slices of pork and behind these as
> counter-basses were two large pigeons, with six ortolans [larks]
> who were the sopranos.

Historian Giuseppe Conti wrote *Facts and Anecdotes of Florentine History*
in 1902. In it, he describes the Company of the Cauldron, or Paiuolo:

> The Company founded by Rustici was that of the Paiuolo.
> The Company of Paiuolo was composed of a party of gentle-
> men who gathered in the room of the Sapienza. At the
> dinners and to pass the time each of the twelve members con-
> ducted no more than four people; and everyone was obliged
> to bring a dinner of his own invention; and if there was found
> two who had had the same idea, they were given a punish-
> ment at the pleasure of the Signore, who was the leader. He
> would then collect the dishes that were brought and redistrib-
> ute them as he liked. As soon as he had formed the Company
> of the Paiuolo, Giovan Francesco Rustici gave a dinner to his
> companions; and to justify the title, brought into the room
> a vat, that was attached to the ceiling by a large handle held
> there by a iron hook, the room was painted and curtains hung
> to add to the effect of them being in an enormous *paiuolo*
> (pot). The companions who had just arrived on the threshold
> were surprised and applauded this strange sight; and enter-
> ing began to laugh like crazy at the vat, where inside were
> seats and in the middle a table. From the ceiling, attached
> by a handle, was hung a chandelier, that lighted the inside
> of the *paiuolo*. When they were all seated, the table opened
> and there appeared a tree with many branches on which were
> ingenuously placed two dishes of the main course for everyone
> of the invited. The tree disappeared when the first dishes were
> finished, and reappeared with others. Around the paiuolo
> were servants, who poured vintage wines. . . .

In 1508, Leonardo was back in Florence, living in the house of his rich
patron, Piero di Braccio Martelli, as was Rustici. Rustici had a menagerie

in his studio consisting of an eagle, a crow "who could speak like a man," snakes, and a porcupine trained like a dog. Leonardo and Rustico were friends, and undoubtedly Leonardo participated in some of the banquets held there. Serge Bramly notes, "Leonardo, himself much given to jokes of all kinds and perhaps the first among artists to possess many animals, must have felt at home in the free and easy atmosphere of the Casa Martelli."

THE VEGETARIAN

Leonardo writes in his notebooks, "Now does not nature produce enough simple [vegetarian] food for you to satisfy yourself? And if you are not content with such, can you not by the mixture of them make infinite compounds, as Platina describes and other writers on food?" These quotes are often given as evidence that Leonardo was a vegetarian, but this is not well known today.

Colin Spencer, author of *The Heretic's Feast: A History of Vegetarianism*, bemoans the fact that Leonardo is not more celebrated as a famous vegetarian. "Yet in the sixty or so biographies in the London Library on his life and work," he writes, "only one book bothers to discuss his vegetarianism." That may be true for the earlier biographies, but the more current ones do discuss it. Nicholl refers to his "famous vegetarianism," and Bramly notes: "There cannot have been many vegetarians in Renaissance Italy."

Sigmund Freud thought that Leonardo was a man torn between pity and aggression. His vegetarianism was part of the "pity" side of him because he didn't like what he thought was cruelty to animals; the "aggression" side of him were his designs of military weapons and, according to Freud, his suppressed sadism from his practice of accompanying condemned criminals to execution so that he could draw their facial expressions upon death.

Although he is sometimes referred to as a lifelong vegetarian, there is considerable evidence that Leonardo ate meat in his early life and probably turned totally vegetarian only in his later years. In the *Codex Leicester*, Leonardo designed a meat-roasting jack, a device for turning a roast, and in *MSS B* of the Library of the Institut de France there is a description of his design of a stove for smoking meats. "And the smoke proceeds to spread itself throughout the numerous flues," Leonardo wrote, "and to cure salted meats, tongues, and sausages to perfection."

Later in life, however, Leonardo seems to have rejected eating meat. According to a Florentine traveler, Andrea Corsali, writing from Cochin,

India, to Giuliano de' Medici, the Gujarati people there "do not feed on anything that has blood, nor will they allow anyone to hurt any living thing, like our Leonardo da Vinci; they live on rice, milk and other inanimate foods." Biographer Eugene Muntz writes in *Leonardo da Vinci: Artist, Thinker, and Man of Science* (1898): "It appears that from Corsali's letter that Leonardo ate no meat, but lived entirely on vegetables, thus forestalling modern vegetarians by several centuries." But what about Leonardo's surviving shopping lists, which include meat? Charles Nicholl notes: "The fact that meat is bought every day does not show that Leonardo was at this point a meat-eater, only that he did not insist on others in his household abstaining."

Some scholars have speculated that Leonardo's life was in danger in fifteenth-century Italy simply because he was a vegetarian. The then-prevailing Catholic orthodoxy held that, because God had given humankind dominion over all the animal kingdom, it was nothing short of blasphemy to refrain from eating flesh. The Church called vegetarian food "the Devil's banquet" and could have burned vegetarians at the stake for heresy. Yet, somehow Leonardo got away with it, just as he got away with other forms of heresy, like his publicly avowed belief in rational science and "humanism" and his arrest (charges later dropped) for sodomy. One of the great mysteries about Leonardo is, in light of his secular views, how he still received commissions and money from the Church. It could be a simple matter of his fame as a painter, or because Leonardo was a hired painter and the Church (and other patrons) wanted him to paint religious scenes.

Leonardo believed God was the *primo motore*, or prime mover, but he attributed the functioning of the world to nature and formulated a religious philosophy that relied more on a respect for life than constant supplication to God. Out of this philosophy evolved his vegetarianism. He could have been burned at the stake for being a heretic, or hanged—but he wasn't.

Leonardo's Salad Dressing

In his notebooks, Leonardo includes what appears to be part of a salad dressing recipe—a list that consists of "parsley (10 parts), mint (1 part), thyme (1 part), vinegar, a little salt." Using this sketchy information as a basis, I have created the following dressing and added olive oil to it. Serve it with a salad Platina-style, consisting of lettuce, mint, fennel, parsley, thyme, and marjoram.

INGREDIENTS

10 teaspoons fresh Italian parsley, minced
1 teaspoon fresh spearmint, minced
1 teaspoon fresh thyme, minced
¾ cup olive oil
¼ cup wine vinegar
Salt and freshly ground black pepper, to taste

Combine all ingredients in a jar and shake well.

YIELD: 1 cup

Zucchine Fritte
(Fried Zucchini with Anise)

This striking vegetarian side is easy to make and is a variation on Martino's and Platina's fried gourds. If you don't care for the licorice taste of the anise seeds, substitute mustard seed.

INGREDIENTS

2 quarts salted water
1 pound zucchini, cut into very thin rounds
¾ cup flour
½ teaspoon salt
¼ cup olive oil
1 tablespoon anise seeds, crushed in a mortar
Juice of ½ lemon

In a pot, bring the water to a boil. Add the zucchini slices and when the water returns to the boil, drain them immediately into a colander. Dry the slices on paper towels.

Place the flour and salt in a bowl and dredge the slices until covered.

Heat the oil in a skillet and cook the slices over medium heat until they are crisp and browned. Drain them on paper towels and in a bowl toss them with the crushed anise seeds and sprinkle them with the lemon juice.

YIELD: 4 servings

Peppered Bread

One of Leonardo's shopping lists contained a note for "peppered bread," which is recreated here. Serve this with olive oil for dipping.

INGREDIENTS

1 package dry yeast
¼ cup hot water
2⅓ cups flour, divided
1 teaspoon salt
2 tablespoons granulated sugar
¼ teaspoon baking soda
1 cup sour cream
1 egg
1 cup grated Parmesan cheese
1 teaspoon freshly ground black pepper

Grease 2 loaf pans. In large mixing bowl, dissolve the yeast in hot water. Add 1⅓ cups of the flour. Add the salt, sugar, baking soda, sour cream, and egg. With a hand beater, blend for 30 seconds on low speed, scraping the bowl constantly. Beat 2 minutes on high speed, scraping the bowl occasionally. Stir in the remaining flour, cheese, and pepper. Divide the batter between the pans. Let it rise in a warm place for 50 minutes. Bake at 350° F for 40 minutes (or until golden brown). Immediately remove from the pans. Cool slightly before slicing.

YIELD: 2 loaves

Cinnamon Tart

Here is a simple tart recipe from fifteenth-century Italy that accords with da Vinci's notion of "supping lightly."

INGREDIENTS

4 egg yolks
2 cups milk
½ teaspoon cinnamon
½ cup sugar
9-inch prebaked pie crust

Preheat the oven to 375° F. In a bowl, combine all the ingredients and beat well with a whisk. Pour into the pie crust and bake for about 1 hour.

YIELD: 6 servings

Brigidini
(Salai's Anise Seed Cookies)

Salai was Giacomo Caprotti, one of Leonardo's assistants and, reputedly, his lover. According to Leonardo's notes, Salai loved "anise sweets," and these cookies are a specialty from Tuscany, Leonardo's childhood home.

INGREDIENTS

1 cup all-purpose flour
Pinch of salt
1 teaspoon double-acting baking powder
7 tablespoons butter at room temperature
3 tablespoons sugar
1 egg
1 teaspoon anise seeds
Milk, as needed

In a bowl, sift together the flour, salt, and baking powder. Mix in the butter thoroughly. Add the sugar, egg, anise seeds, and just enough milk to bind the mixture into a firm dough. Knead the dough well on a floured board and shape into nut-sized balls. Flatten them with a spatula and cook, a few at a time, on a greased hot griddle or in a heavy skillet until golden brown.

YIELD: 6 servings

Chapter Six

Fantastic Feasts

Some of the greatest legacies of Renaissance Italy are the banquets and spectacles produced by rulers of the city-states to impress their contemporaries and the populace, as well. These banquets had social, political, and religious significance that varied in importance according to the status of the host and the specific reason for the celebration.

The Great Banquets of Italy

As medieval times evolved into the Renaissance, several different factors radically changed the banquet in the Italian city-states. First was the resurgence of interest in classical authors who described the banquets of ancient Rome, which, of course, celebrated pagan gods or mythological nuptial feasts such as that of Cupid and Psyche. Next was a movement toward culinary abundance rather than restraint; food historian Roy Strong describes the banquets as "a cornucopia of fruit, flowers, splendid tableware, and rich food." Finally, conversation and spectacle entered the banquet picture. Such events first mirrored those of the ancients, and the *Odes* of Horace were read and later discussed. Then musicians and dancers were added, and, as we shall see, the banquet became a complete spectacle. So complete that, in some of them, the general public was admitted not to eat, but to be an audience for the entire event. This, of course, was the precursor of reality TV, but here the commoners were allowed an intimate view of the life of the court.

Traditional feast days governed by the church calendar, says historian Serge Bramly, "lost their pious character and increasingly tended to be pure spectacle." Christmas, All Saints' Day, Carnival, May Day, and the

Royal banquet, c. 1450
North Wind Picture Archives

Feast of St. John were filled with dances, games, promotional exhibits (like a modern trade show), floats, horse races, and fights among wild animals. Yes, it sounds like the spectacles in the Coliseum in ancient Rome. These spectacles required design, costuming, machinery, and stage direction—talents possessed by Leonardo.

Let's take a look at some of the more memorable Italian banquets held in Leonardo's time. In June 1466, at the wedding uniting the Rucellai and Medici families in Florence, a huge tent was erected opposite the palace. On one side of the tent there was a sideboard containing silver vessels and gold dishes produced by the finest smiths in the city. On the other side of the tent was the kitchen, where fifty cooks and helpers labored to prepare a magnificent banquet. Servants carried presents from the friends, clients, and relations of the two families, pipers and trumpeters were practicing their music, and the cavaliers were preparing for the tilting match. The Via della Vigna was completely filled with guests and onlookers, and the noise was deafening.

Finally, the food was ready to be served: quartered bullocks, casks of Greek wine, capons hung up on a staff carried by two strong peasants, huge bars of buffalo cheese, roasted fowl, barrels of local ordinary wine and fine sweet wine, hampers of sea fish, baskets full of pomegranates, and baskets full of sweetmeats, tarts, and confectionaries prepared by nuns.

Looking at the wedding of Lorenzo di Piero di Cosimo to Clarice Orsini in Florence on June 4, 1469, we get an idea of the extravagant way the dishes were presented. Piero di Marco Parenti, a writer who witnessed the event, describes the scene:

> No sideboards had been placed for the silver. Only tall tables in the middle of the courtyard, round that handsome column on which stands the David [Donatello's *David*] covered with tablecloths, and at the four corners were four great copper basins for the glasses, and behind the tables stood men to hand over the wine or water to those who served the guests. On the tables were silver vessels in which the glasses were put to be kept cool. The salt cellars, forks, knife-handles, bowls for the fritters, almonds, sugar-plums, and the jars for preserved pine-seeds were of silver; there was none other for the guests save the basins and jugs for washing of hands. The tablecloths were of the finest white damask linen laid according to our fashion.

MENU FOR THE TRIVULZIO-D'ARAGONA
WEDDING FEAST, 1488

1. Rose water for the hands
   Pastries with pine nuts and sugar
   Other cakes made with almonds and sugar
2. Asparagus
3. Tiny sausages and meatballs
4. Roast grey partridge and sauce
5. Whole calves heads, gilded and silvered
6. Capons and pigeons, accompanied by sausages, hams, and wild boar, plus delicate potages
7. Whole roast sheep, with a sour cherry sauce
8. A great variety of roast birds: doves, partridges, pheasants, quail, and figpeckers, with olives
9. Chickens with sugar and rose water
10. Whole roast suckling pig
11. Roast peacock, with various accompaniments
12. A mixture of eggs, milk, sage, and flour
13. Quinces cooked with sugar, cinnamon, pine nuts, and artichokes
14. Various preserves, made with sugar and honey
15. Ten different torte, and an abundance of candied spice

In 1473, the wedding of Eleanora of Aragon, daughter of Ferdinand I of Naples, to Ercole I, the duke of Ferrara, was held outdoors in Rome in front of the cardinal's palace. A three-room gallery was built outside with a fabric ceiling and luxurious tapestries decorating the rooms. It lasted seven hours, featured gold cutlery, and the entertainment was a series of mythological fantasies referring to the bride and groom as Jason and Medea, Bacchus and Ariadne, and Hercules and Deianira. This was the beginning of the allegorical banquet; fake battles were staged, castles made of sugar were broken up and thrown to the guests, and at one point Venus appeared in a chariot pulled by two "swans."

In another allegorical marriage banquet, that of Costanzo Sforza to Camilla d'Aragona at Pesaro in 1475, the nuptials were supervised by the gods of Mount Olympus. The hot dishes were served in the sun (Apollo supervising) and the cold dishes by moonlight (Diana supervising). A similar allegorical banquet was given in 1484 by Ascanio Sforza in honor of the prince of Capua. In that extravaganza, eight courses were served by

Olympic gods: Venus, Jupiter, and Juno served the roast dishes, and Neptune, of course, served the fish dishes from a marine chariot.

In 1488, Ludovico's enemy, Gian Giacomo Trivulzio, married Beatrice d'Aragona in Milan, and we actually have a menu for the banquet (see sidebar on previous page). Trivulzio was a condottiere, an elite mercenary leader. Ironically, in 1506, Leonardo did a series of drawings for Trivulzio's tomb. However, the project, which featured Trivulzio mounted on a huge horse (sound familiar?) never got beyond the planning stages.

By 1490, Leonardo had two titles at the Sforza court: *ingeniarius ducalis*, or "duke's engineer," and *ingeniarius camerarius*, or "room engineer," an allusion to the production of elaborate festivals. In January of that same year, Ludovico threw a huge banquet called *Il Paradiso*, or the "Feast of Paradise," and invited diplomats and state leaders from all across Italy. The menu for the food has not survived, as many observers were more interested in the spectacle, of which Leonardo was the head producer. We do not know if he planned the feasting, but he did produce the climax of the evening, which was called "The Masque of the Planets." The event required a small army of designers, workmen, painters, and actors. After the feasting came the dancing, and then at midnight the music stopped, and Ludovico, dressed in an oriental costume, gave the cue, and the curtain was raised on Leonardo's "The Masque of the Planets." Michael White describes it as "a giant model of the planets in their respective positions, each moving on its course with the signs of the zodiac illuminated by torches placed behind colored glass."

Biographer Charles Nicholl comments:

> *Il Paradiso* shows us Leonardo the courtly spectaculist, the special-effects man. It was the multimedia extravaganza of its day—physically constructed of wood and cloth, transformed and animated into something ethereal by a combination of color, lighting, music, ballet, and poetry. The show was reprised later in the year for another high-society wedding.

Ironically for Leonardo, it was "The Masque of the Planets" that made him famous all over Italy, not his paintings. The guests left Milan feeling that they had seen the finest entertainment of their lives, and they spread the word that the greatest genius in the land lived at the Sforza court, and he was Leonardo the Florentine. Most scholars think that Ludovico believed this, too.

CITY OF CITRUS

"In 1529, the Archbishop of Milan gave a sixteen-course dinner that included caviar and oranges fried with sugar and cinnamon, brill and sardines with slices of orange and lemon, one thousand oysters with pepper and oranges, lobster salad with citrons, sturgeon in aspic covered with orange juice, fried sparrows with oranges, individual salads containing citrons into which the coat of arms had been carved, orange fritters, a soufflé full of raisins and pine nuts and covered with sugar and orange juice, five hundred fried oysters with lemon slices, and candied peels of citrons and oranges."

—John McPhee, *Oranges*

Contemporary accounts of the 1491 wedding feast and festivities revolving around Ludovico's marriage to Beatrice d'Este reveal that Leonardo did indeed have the servants in costume, dressed as "wild men," or *omini salvatichi*. The wild man was a popular folkloric figure of the time, usually pictured dressed in animal skins or leaves and bark and carrying a large club—we would say "caveman" today. Leonardo designed the costumes, and Roy Strong writes about one account of the event, which included a jousting match, describes "a great company of men on horses, accoutred like wild men, with huge drums and raucous trumpets."

Roy Strong notes another account that describes a procession of 103 men carrying "tigers, unicorns, bucentaurs, foxes, wolves, lions…mountains, dromedaries, lobsters, castle Saracens, children, the Columns of Hercules, Hercules killing the dragon, lynxes, sheep, bucks, elephants, men at arms, large lilies, eagles, chained hounds, vases, and many other things, all painted and made life-size of solid sugar." It is not clear if Leonardo made the sugar sculptures or directed their creation, but it would seem likely that he had something to do with them, considering his exalted position in the court. Whatever the case, the audience expressed its delight by getting out of hand and smashing the sculptures, much to the displeasure of Ludovico. The Venetian ambassadors, Zaccaria Barbaro and Francesco Capello, brought as many as 150 persons in their suite, and the duke's steward records that upwards of 45,000 pounds of meat were consumed at court during that week.

A second type of feast, after the allegorical court feast, was the theme feast. At the Feast of St. Andrew, produced by the Cazzuola, or Company of the Trowel, in the summer of 1512 in Florence, guests came dressed in

The Wedding Feast, by Sandro Botticelli, 1483
Sunbelt Archives

their workmens' and builders' clothes and carried their trowels and hammers. In the first room, the producer of the event showed them the plan of a building they were to construct. He then placed the masons at the main table, and the workmen began to bring in the trays of lasagne and ricotta with sugar, to lay the foundations for the building.

The mortar consisted of cheeses and spices to flavor the lasagne, and for the gravel, pieces of ring cake were used. The building-blocks were flat loaves of bread that served as tiles. The building was constructed using these materials, and when it seemed to the masons that all the work had been done in accordance with the rules of construction and art, the twenty-four workers gleefully demolished the building and began eating the foundation, in which they found cakes and small pieces of pig's liver.

Then, a tall column of Parmesan cheese, wrapped in cooked veal tripe, was brought in, and as the workers began to dismantle the column to eat it, inside they found roast capons, veal liver, and spiced tongue to further stuff themselves with. But there was more! After the column, a section of lintel, frieze, and cornice was brought in for dessert. As one witness observed: "So when they had filled their bodies, the noise and the songs began, and a play was performed. This was how the Cazzuola held its meetings every year." Leonardo would have loved it! But alas, he was back in Milan at the time.

COURT JESTER

Some of the dukes who ran the Renaissance Italian courts had a wicked sense of humor and even played practical food jokes. An author who was a contemporary of Leonardo's, Sabadino degli Arienti, wrote that Ercole d'Este, duke of Ferrara, conned a peasant named Bondeno, who had the audacity to apply to become a knight. D'Este granted him the knighthood and arranged for the ceremony. With trumpets blaring and the crowd howling with laughter, the new "knight's" shield bearing his coat of arms was revealed: a head of garlic on a blue background! This demonstration illustrated the impossibility of crossing social lines because garlic had such a lowly status at the time.

Another innovative theme dinner of the Company of the Trowel involved the guests going straight to hell. The theme was: Ceres is seeking her daughter Proserpine in Hades, but Pluto refuses to give her up, instead throwing a nuptial feast where the guests arrive through a door that is a snake's mouth. Giorgio Vasari, Leonardo's early biographer, describes the event:

> [They] find themselves in a round room illuminated by one
> small light in the middle, so that they scarcely recognize each
> other. They are shown into their places at the black-draped
> table by a hideous devil holding a fork, and Pluto commands
> that the pains of hell shall cease so long as they remain there,
> in honor of the wedding. The viands were all animals of the
> most repulsive appearance but with the delicate means of
> various kinds underneath. The exteriors were serpents, toads,
> lizards, newts, spiders, frogs, scorpions, bats, and such things,
> with the most delicious viands inside. They were placed
> before each guest with a fire-shovel, and a devil poured choice
> wines from an ugly glass horn.... Instead of fruits, dead men's
> bones followed...but they were made of sugar.

A third type of Renaissance feast, the private banquet, was also quite popular. On May 20, 1529, Ippolito d'Este, the archbishop of Milan, hosted a party for his brother Ercole at the d'Este palace of Belfiore. The festive occasion with fifty-four guests began in the early evening outdoors with mounted men charging a target with lances—a traditional chivalrous exercise. At nine o'clock, the guests moved into one of the frescoed halls to

Lady of quality dining, c. 1460
North Wind Picture Archives

view the performance of a farce and a concert, which lasted for an hour. Then it was back to the gardens. Surrounded by flowers and greenery was a large center table with two service tables on either side, one for the food and another for the wine. Across from the tables were the musicians, for music was the uniting theme of the banquet.

On the table were tablecloths, and usually only two were used—one on top for the main courses and one beneath for the final fruit course. But at this banquet, an astounding eighteen tablecloths were used—one for each course. The guests were led to the table from the palace by wandering minstrels and dancing young men and women. They then washed their hands in perfumed water, were seated, and began the first course, which, in addition to the traditional bread rolls, included antipasti of cold dishes and salads, for a total of eight dishes. The second course had a fish theme and consisted of trout patties, sturgeon roe, pike spleens, and other fish flavored with orange, cinnamon, and sugar, plus boiled sturgeon with garlic and fried bream.

TO PRESENT PEACOCKS IN ALL THEIR PLUMAGE, WHICH THOUGH COOKED, APPEAR ALIVE, SPOUTING FIRE FROM THEIR BEAKS

This recipe is typical of the theatrics of an Italian Renaissance wedding feast. It is from Maestro Martino in 1465 and is presented in its original form since it probably would not be prepared by any reader of this book. Interestingly, Alice Waters of the Chez Panisse restaurant in Berkeley, California, attempted a similar dish around 1975 and suggested replacing the peacock's eyes with moonstones. Platina plagiarized this recipe almost word for word in his volume.

To prepare lifelike peacocks in their feathers: first the peacock must be killed, either with a quill which is thrust into the top of its head, or by bleeding it from the throat like a kid. Then cut it open from throat to tail, piercing just the skin and peeling it off carefully so that neither skin nor feathers are damaged. When you have skinned the body, pull the skin of the neck inside out over the head, which you then detach from the top of the neck, while leaving it connected just by the skin. Do the same with the legs, which you sever from the carcass, while leaving them attached to the skin of the drumsticks. Now prepare the skinned bird neatly, stuffed with good things and mild spices, and take whole cloves and stick them into the flesh of the breast. Roast it slowly on the spit, with a damp cloth around the neck so that it does not dry out in the heat of the fire, moistening the cloth continually. When the peacock is cooked, take it off the spit and put it back in its skin. Now take a metal contraption fixed to a wooden base in such a way that iron rods pass through the feet and legs of the bird without being visible, so that the peacock stands bolt upright, head erect, as if it were alive, tail feathers carefully fanned out like the spokes of a wheel. If you want it to spit fire from its beak, take a quarter of an ounce of camphor wrapped in some wadding lint [cotton] and put it in the peacock's mouth with some strong spirits [grappa] or fortified wine as well. When you are ready to send the bird to the table, set the wadding alight and it will burn for quite some time. For even greater magnificence, cover the cooked bird with sheets of gold leaf before putting it back in its skin, which will have been coated on the inside with mild spices. This can also be done with pheasants, cranes, geese, and other birds, or capons and poultry.

Course after course was served while the guests listened to lute solos, madrigals, songs by French girls, and other musical entertainment. In fact, each course had its own musical theme, and the sturgeon arrived to music from three trumpets and three cornets. The entire resources of the d'Este court were displayed, from the elaborate, meat-free courses (it was a day of abstinence) to the spectacle of dance to the wide variety of musical style. The entire affair came to an end at five o'clock in the morning.

We know in great detail of this banquet because of Cristoforo Messisbugo's book *Banchetti, composizioni di vivande e apparecchio generale* of 1549, which had thirteen editions published up to 1626. The success of the book shows how fascinated the people were with the fashionable and exclusive d'Este court—and, indeed the other courts of the time and the recent past.

FLUTTERING PIE

Here is another spectacular banquet recipe from Maestro Martino. Sometimes baby rabbits were used in place of the birds.

Make a large pie crust with a hole at the bottom as big as your fist or bigger, making the sides higher than usual. Fill the container with flour and bake in the oven. When done, empty out the flour, take the pie crust out of its container, and insert another pie, small enough to go through the hole, already cooked and full of good things. Just before serving, fill the space between the large and small pies with live birds of whatever kind you can get and, when the lid is opened up at the table, the birds will fly out, to the amusement and delight of the guests. But so as not to disappoint them, hand around slices of the small pie. You could make as many of these as you please, or in the shape of a tart, adjusting things accordingly.

But there was an occasional voice of protest about the lavish court banquets. Luigi Cornaro, who was roughly contemporary with Leonardo (c. 1465–1566), was a nobleman in Venice and led a life of great indulgence until he was thirty-five and his health broke down. He completely changed his ways and started a diet of vegetables, dry bread, and water. He lived to be 101. In an essay entitled "Gluttony Murders," he rants about overindulgence:

> O wretched and unhappy Italy! Can you not see that gluttony
> murders every year more of your inhabitants than you could
> lose by the most cruel plague or by fire and sword in many
> battles. Those truly shameful feasts, now so much in fashion
> and so intolerably profuse that no tables are large enough to

hold the infinite number of dishes—those feasts, I say, are so many battles....Put an end to this abuse, in heaven's name, for there is not—I am certain of it—a vice more abominable than this in the eyes of the divine Majesty.

But of course, the popes and dukes weren't listening to Luigi.

The influence of the Italian court kitchens and banquets has been debated endlessly, particularly the contention that Italian Renaissance food had a profound influence on the cuisine of France.

CATHERINE, THE ARTICHOKE QUEEN

Catherine de' Medici, of the famed banking family in Florence and the eventual queen of France, was born fifteen days before Leonardo died in 1519. In 1533, when she was just fourteen, she married the heir to the French Crown, the duke of Orleans, Henry de Valois, who was crowned Henry II in 1547. Italian food expert Anna Maria Volpi tells the traditional story about Catherine's culinary influence on the French court:

> When she moved to France, a crowd of friends, servants, and waiters accompanied her. The Florentine cooks who went with her brought the secrets of Italian cooking to France, including peas and beans, artichokes, duck in orange (*canard a l'orange*), and *carabaccia* (onion soup). But especially the pastry makers, as Jean Orieux (a biographer of Caterina) wrote, demonstrated their innovative genius with sorbets and ice creams, marmalades, fruits in syrup, pastry making, and pasta. A certain Sir Frangipani gave his name to the custard and the tart known in France as *Frangipane*.

Cookbook historian L. Patrick Coyle adds:

> What were some specific items of cuisine? Pasta, milk-fed veal covered with a light sauce, crisp broccoli, *piselli novelli* (later dubbed *petits pois*). Truffles, juicy tournedos, quenelles, ice cream, rice pudding, kidneys, sweetbreads, cocks' combs, "royal carp," zabiglione (called *sayabon* in France), macaroons, and frangipane tarts.

The influence of Catherine on the French pasta experience is almost a certainty, because Catherine's wedding banquet included one savory dish

Catherine de' Medici, 1519–1589
North Wind Picture Archives

of pasta with the juice of a meat roast and topped with cheese and another sweet one flavored with butter, sugar, honey, saffron, and cinnamon.

Artichokes were Catherine's favorite vegetable. Supposedly, she scandalized society by eating it, as it was thought to be an aphrodisiac. Perhaps it was for her, as she had nine children. It is likely that her entourage introduced artichokes into France, as they were transferred from Naples to Florence in 1466 and were growing in France in the mid-sixteenth century. Catherine arrived in 1533.

It is also possible that Catherine introduced broccoli, because the vegetable had close links to Italy. The Romans ate it, and the word "broccoli" in Italian means "little arms" or "little sprouts." Also, there is a broccoli variety called "Calabrese," suggesting an origin in Calabria. Waverly Root writes that Catherine's cooks indeed introduced broccoli into France because the first French use of the word *brocoli* is dated to 1560.

Also possible is the transference of peas from Italy to France, because the sixteenth century is given as the date for their introduction into Europe. Root agrees with Coyle that Catherine's staff transferred the tiny sweet peas, called *piselli novelli* in Italian, which were translated as *petits pois* in French. However, it is unlikely that the Florentines taught the French to love truffles, since fifteenth-century sources report about muzzled pigs being used in France to dig for them.

Pastries were relatively new in Florence when Catherine left, but her cooks could have brought recipes with them. *Torta balconata*, a cake in tiers, was one of the favorite desserts, and it contained almonds and candied fruits. Some sources credit her court with introducing the separation of salty dishes and sweet dishes during dining; apparently the French were still eating sweets with meat in the medieval manner.

Her court is reputed to have introduced recipes such as *pintade à la Medicis* (Stuffed Guinea Hen, Medici-Style) and a carp dish first known as Royal Carp and finally as Carp of the House of France. It became a traditional dish of the French royal family. Another recipe said to be introduced was *anatra all'apicio*, a duck stuffed with herbs, garlic, and vinegar, which was grilled on a spit and served with bitter orange juice. One online source claims that she introduced asparagus into France, but Alan Davidson, in *The Oxford Companion to Food*, gives 1469 as the arrival date for asparagus in France, fully sixty-four years before Catherine arrived.

The question is not whether or not Catherine introduced Florentine foods, recipes, and techniques to the French court, but rather what influence Catherine's court had on the future of French cuisine. There could

Artichoke
Sunbelt Archives

be something of the *post hoc* fallacy here. *Post hoc ergo propter hoc* translates into "after this therefore because of this" and indicates the fallacy of a cause-and-effect assertion based on a chronological sequence of events.

Food historian Reay Tannahill is dismissive of the claims that Catherine's cooks had a major influence on French cooking. She writes, "But, as so often with the kind of history that is built on anecdote, this was an optimistic version of reality." But the fact remains that many of the cooking precepts of the Florentine cooks reappear in one of the most important early French cookbooks, *Le cuisinier francois*, written by Pierre Francois de la Varenne and published in 1651. This book was so popular that it went through thirty editions in the following seventy-five years. Instead of featuring the intense spicing of meats popular during medieval times, Varenne emphasized reducing stocks and sauces to add more flavor and promoted vegetables such as asparagus, broccoli, cauliflower, artichokes, and green peas.

Italian food expert Anna Del Conte comments:

> How much of this change was due to Caterina de' Medici and her oft-reported (but never proved) retinue of cooks is highly debatable, as is the contribution made to French haute cuisine by another Medici, Maria, half a century or so later when she

Serving utensils, c. 1610
North Wind Picture Archives

married Henry IV. Certainly the introduction into France of the lavishness and refinement of the Italian court was partly due to these two queens.

Maguelonne Toussaint-Samat, the French author of *History of Food*, has twelve references to Catherine in her book, and one of them refers to the queen as "gluttonous." One of Catherine's favorite foods was "cock's kidneys and combs fried with artichoke bottoms," and during one feast, she ate so much of this dish that "she thought she would die," according to chronicler Pierre de L' Estoile. Toussaint-Samat agrees with the historians who believe that Catherine's retinue had an effect on French cuisine, writing: "The Medici queens of France...brought with them to their new country...Italian virtuosi who had a great influence on French cooking, particularly in the art of concocting desserts and working with sugar." One of those desserts was sorbet, from the Italian *sorbetto*. Catherine's entourage introduced such flavored ices at Catherine's wedding cebration, and the new queen had a different flavored ice for each day of her celebration in 1533. By 1576 there were 250 master icemakers in Paris. Ice from the mountains was brought to Paris and stored in icehouses; eventually there was a large ice depot situated, appropriately enough, on the Rue de la Glaciere.

Interestingly, in 1549, the city of Paris gave a dinner to honor Catherine, and the menu consisted mostly of birds (the most prized meat of Renaissance Florence), including thirty peacocks, twenty-one swans, nine cranes, thirty-three herons, thirty-three night herons, and thirty-three egrets.

SHARING THE FOOD

In June 1469, on the occasion of his marriage to Clarice Orsini, Lorenzo the Magnificent distributed to the Florentines, from the palazzo in Via Larga, the huge gifts of food that he had received. On the day of the ceremony, the people were not offered the usual leftovers but 1,500 wooden serving boards of chickens, fish, sugared almonds, and other delicious treats.

Veal with Prosciutto and Raisins

Veal was the preferred form of beef in Renaissance Italy, and it works well in this combination dish, which was originally published in *Cuoco napolitano* (*The Cook of Naples*). The addition of the eggs at the end of the cooking is unusual but tasty. Serve with risotto.

INGREDIENTS

1 tablespoon olive oil
1 medium onion, finely chopped
¼ pound prosciutto, minced
1 pound veal, coarsely minced
1 teaspoon ground ginger
1 teaspoon ground cinnamon
3 tablespoons golden raisins
½ cup chicken stock
3 eggs
½ cup grape juice mixed with 1 tablespoon red wine vinegar (verjuice)
Freshly ground black pepper, to taste

Heat the oil in a large skillet and sauté the onion until it is soft. Add the prosciutto and veal and cook over medium heat, stirring occasionally, until the veal loses its pinkness, about 7 minutes. Add the ginger, cinnamon, black pepper, raisins, and stock and cook, uncovered, over medium heat for 12 minutes, stirring occasionally. The liquid should all be evaporated or absorbed.

In a bowl, combine the eggs and the verjuice mixture and beat with a whisk. Add to the pan, stirring constantly, until the eggs have set. Serve immediately.

YIELD: 4 servings

Roasted Pork Loin with Apple and Leek Sauce

Roasts were considered the featured foods at banquets, and the pork served was usually a whole suckling pig. Since that particular dish is difficult to prepare at home, here is a more manageable pork loin.

INGREDIENTS

2 teaspoons fresh rosemary, minced, or 1 teaspoon dried rosemary,
  crushed
1 clove garlic, minced
1 teaspoon olive oil
2-pound boneless pork top loin roast
1 cup apple juice
1 medium leek, chopped
1 small apple, peeled, cored, and chopped
2 teaspoons cornstarch
2 tablespoons white wine vinegar
Salt and freshly ground black pepper

Preheat the oven to 325° F.

In a bowl, combine the rosemary, garlic, and olive oil. Rub this mixture over the roast. Place the roast on a rack in a shallow roasting pan. Roast, uncovered, for 1½ hours or until the internal temperature reaches 160° F. Transfer roast to a warm serving platter and keep warm in the oven. Reserve 2 tablespoons of the pan drippings.

In a saucepan bring ¾ cup of the apple juice to a boil. Add leek and apple; reduce heat. Cover and simmer for 4 minutes or just until tender. Combine the remaining ¼ cup apple juice and the cornstarch and stir to blend. Add this to the leek mixture. Stir in reserved pan drippings, vinegar, salt, and pepper. Cook and stir until thickened. Cook and stir for 2 minutes more.

To serve, cut the roast into slices and cover with the sauce.

YIELD: 6 to 8 servings

Sausages Braised in Wine with Vegetables

Despite being considered something of a peasant dish, some sausages make appearances on many banquet menus. This flavorful dish combines them with carrots, onions, and celery.

INGREDIENTS

3 tablespoons butter
3 carrots, finely chopped
2 onions, finely chopped
2 ribs celery, finely chopped
2 tablespoons olive oil
4 Italian sausages, pricked
3 cloves
2 bay leaves
½ cup Chianti

In a Dutch oven, melt the butter and sauté the carrots, onions, and celery until they are soft. Remove from the pot and reserve. Add the olive oil and the sausages and sauté over low heat until the sausages are brown, about 10 minutes. Return the vegetables to the pot, add the remaining ingredients, and cover and cook on low heat for 30 minutes.

YIELD: 4 to 6 servings

Saffron Risotto with Duck and Mushrooms

Here is a favorite banquet dish that was served at the court of Mantua during Leonardo's time. Originally, truffles were used instead of the mushrooms, but today's cost makes that impossible. Mushrooms were on one of Leonardo's shopping lists, so it's a good bet that he ate them. Serve this with a garden salad and tossed with an olive oil-based dressing.

INGREDIENTS

6 tablespoons butter
3 medium onions, 2 chopped and 1 minced
10 cloves garlic, 8 halved and 2 minced
1 duck, cleaned and sectioned into pieces
1¼ cups dry Italian white wine
½ teaspoon salt
¼ teaspoon freshly ground pepper
8 whole cloves
2 dried porcini mushrooms, rehydrated in warm water, chopped
2 cups long grain rice
4 cups chicken stock
2 pinches saffron soaked in ¼ cup water
1 cup button mushrooms, thinly sliced

In a heavy casserole, melt 4 tablespoons of the butter and sauté the 2 chopped onions and 16 garlic halves until they just turn brown. Add the duck pieces and fry until they just turn brown. Add the wine, reduce the heat, and add the salt, pepper, cloves, and the porcini mushrooms, then cook, covered, over low heat for about 2 hours or until the meat starts to fall off the bone.

Remove the duck pieces and bone them, then cut the meat into ½-inch pieces. Remove the garlic halves and discard them. Remove any fat from the pan and return the meat to the juices.

Heat the remaining butter in a large skillet and cook the minced onion and garlic until golden. Add the rice and stir constantly for 1 minute, then add the stock and the saffron water. Bring to a boil, reduce the heat, and cook for 15 minutes, or until all the liquid has been absorbed.

To serve, arrange the rice in a ring around a serving dish and cover it with the sliced mushrooms. Pile the meat with the juices in the center of the ring.

YIELD: 6 servings

Catherine's Sorbetto alla Arancia
(Orange Sorbet)

Of course, we have no specific recipe extant from Catherine's food adventures in France, but here's a guess.

INGREDIENTS

½ cup sugar
2 cups orange juice
½ teaspoon orange rind, finely grated
1 egg white, beaten
Fresh mint leaves for garnish

Combine the sugar, orange juice, and orange rind in a pan and bring to a boil. Reduce the heat and simmer for 5 minutes, stirring until all the sugar is dissolved. Pour the mixture into a bowl and place in the refrigerator. When cool, add the beaten egg white and stir to mix well. Place in a plastic container in the freezer and stir the mixture once an hour for 3 hours. When frozen, spoon out the sorbet and serve garnished with mint leaves.

YIELD: 4 servings

Chapter Seven

A CUISINE TRIUMPHANT

W hy is Italian food arguably the most popular cuisine in the world? I believe the answer reflects not only the culinary advances of the Italian Renaissance but also the many developments that followed. Of primary significance to the emergence of the modern cuisine of Italy was the discovery of the New World and its exotic foods.

THE COLUMBUS TRANSFER

In 1492, when Leonardo was in the Sforza court in Milan painting and producing lavish court entertainments, his countryman, Christopher Columbus, sailed to the Western Hemisphere and was busy collecting plants (among other things) that he brought back to Spain. Later Spanish conquerors of Mexico followed his lead, importing tomatoes and other unique crops. From Spain and Portugal, traders carried seeds to many ports of call, and tomatoes, peppers, potatoes, maize, and some squash and beans spread around Europe and the world, eventually transforming many cuisines.

The tomato was the most important New World crop transferred to Italy, although it took hundreds of years for it to be accepted into the cuisines. The most logical theory for its transference to Italy holds that the Spaniards, who were in Mexico in the early 1500s, brought it to Spain, and it was transferred to the kingdom of Naples, which came under Spanish control in 1522. From there, it would have spread into the upper peninsula. First it was an ornamental plant because people thought it might be poisonous, like the Solanums it is related to in the nightshade family. The herbalist P. A. Mattioli described a tomato as the "pomo d'oro" or "apple of gold" in 1544 because of its yellow color; this tomato was

The tomato revolutionized pasta sauces in Italy.
Sunbelt Archives

probably about the size of a cherry. Mattioli mentioned a red tomato in 1554. Tomatoes were probably used first in Spanish cooking, and a painting by Bartolome Esteban Murillo, *The Angels' Kitchen*, done in 1646 for the Franciscan convent in Seville, shows angels preparing a meal with tomatoes and eggplants.

The first tomato recipe in an Italian cookbook appeared in Antonio Latini's *Lo scalco alla moderna* (*The Modern Steward*, 1692–1694) for Spanish-Style Tomato Sauce, which called for roasted, peeled, and chopped tomatoes combined with finely chopped parsley, wild thyme, onion, garlic, salt, pepper, oil, and vinegar. Francesco Gaudentio included a recipe called *Il modo di cuocere li pomi d'oro* (The Way to Cook the Tomato) in his book *Il panunto Toscano* (*The Tuscan Bread*), which was published in 1705: "These fruits, which in some ways resemble apples," he writes, "are grown in gardens and can be cooked as follows: Take them, chop them up, and put them in a skillet with olive oil, pepper, salt, minced garlic, and sprigs of mint. Sauté them, stirring them about frequently, and should you want to add some sliced zucchini or eggplant they'll go quite well."

In 1786, Vincenzo Corrado, author of *Il cuoco galante* (*The Gallant Cook*), which was published in Naples, wrote: "Tomatoes, too, are very tasty, and it is a pleasure to observe them so red and plump, peeled and seeded, stuffed and fried." He presented the best collection of tomato recipes so far. Tomatoes are stuffed with veal, stuffed with butter, stuffed with herbs, stuffed with rice, mixed with seafood, and used in croquettes and fritters. His recipe for *pomodori alla napolitana* is still prepared today: tomatoes are stuffed with anchovies, parsley, oregano, and garlic and are sprinkled with bread crumbs and baked in the oven. He makes a pudding this way: "Take the flesh of the tomatoes and puree it with butter and spices and then blend it up with parmesan cheese, bread crumbs and powdered cinnamon. Mix in egg yolks, sweet cream and chopped candied fruits and a bit of sugar to make a flavorful cream; bake it in the oven until firm in a buttered casserole dish, dusted with bread crumbs."

By the end of the eighteenth century, the tomato was firmly established in Italian home cooking. By the middle of the nineteenth century, the tomato was the foundation of sauces in restaurants, too, and the various tomato sauces were served over meats and pastas to a variety of clientele based, as usual, on wealth. But it is significant that pasta sauces in various incarnations were served to the poor, middle class, and aristocracy alike—that's the degree to which tomatoes had infiltrated the Italian cuisine.

In 1875, tomatoes were first cultivated strictly for processing into tomato paste (*concentrato*) near Parma, and commercial production and canning of tomatoes followed in the Naples area. Today, tomato canning and processing is one of Italy's largest agro-industries.

It took an equally long time for peppers to have any impact on Italian cuisine. They first appeared in Italy in 1526, which indicates that they were transferred about the same time as tomatoes were, which makes sense because of Spain's control over Naples at the time. Antonio Latini

Chile peppers added heat to southern Italian foods.
Sunbelt Archives

briefly mentioned them as an ingredient in some sauces, and a century later Vincenzo Corrado called peppers a "vulgar, rustic food." It wasn't until the nineteenth century that pickled peppers were mentioned; however, in the twentieth century, chile peppers called *peperoncini* were grown extensively in the regions of Calabria and Senise, where they have gradually suffused the local cuisine.

Similarly, the potato was virtually ignored until the famines of the eighteenth century in Italy. During that time, the authorities launched a publicity campaign to convince the peasants to eat the "white truffles," as potatoes were often called. The potato's first use was as a flour to be used in baking or in making dumplings. The earliest explication of the culinary usage of potatoes was in Corrado's *The Gallant Cook* in 1786, in which he offers more than fifty different ways to cook with them. Still, the main method he recommends is mixing potato flour with wheat flour to bake bread. Potatoes were (and still are) eaten primarily in northern Italy, where they are stewed and cooked in *tiela di pesce*, a fish pie. But as Waverly Root observes, "Even today, the Italians have not really taken the potato to their bosoms." Possibly, the Italian indifference to potatoes is the result of the tuber's failure to live up to its initial reputation as an aphrodisiac.

The Amazing Story of Maize in Italy

The word "corn" was a generic term in Europe that referred to whichever grain was the primary crop in a given place—so "corn" could mean barley or wheat, which makes a lot of references to "corn" suspect in older sources. Maize is a much more precise term, as it specifically refers to the species *Zea mays* L. and all its hybrids—specifically, New World corn.

There is little doubt that Christopher Columbus returned to Europe with New World maize in 1493. However, a few scholars believe that maize was already growing in Europe and Africa at the time. In 1494, maize was

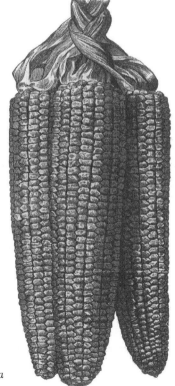

introduced into Italy by the cardinal Ascanio Sforza, brother of Leonardo's patron, Ludovico Sforza, after he was given the seeds by the diplomat and historian Pietro Martire d'Anghiera, also known as Peter Martyr, who received them directly from Columbus.

In the fall of 1495, in the Sforza court at Milan, while working on *The Last Supper*, Leonardo wrote in his notebook a shopping list that included "white maize" and "red maize." It is difficult to confuse this with any other grain because he also mentions millet, buckwheat, and wheat. The word used for maize is *melica*, which in Latin means sorghum, but in Italian means maize.

Maize, the final incarnation of polenta
Sunbelt Archives

The appearance of maize in Leonardo's notebook just over two years after Columbus brought it back raises a number of questions. Was Leonardo referring to the maize seeds of Ascanio Sforza, or was maize already established as a crop near Milan? If we accept the first possibility, what was Leonardo doing with the maize seeds, along with the beans, millet, buckwheat, and peas that are mentioned? If maize was an established crop, did that really happen in only two growing seasons, 1494 and 1495? Was there enough time to plant the few seeds, do a seed increase in 1494, and have a significant crop in 1495? And another question begs to be answered: did Ludovico Sforza encourage the planting of maize like he did the planting of rice, and is that one of the reasons that Lombardy became the largest maize-producing region in Italy and the center of the love of polenta?

Or, was maize already established in some parts of Europe? Interestingly, in 1498, Vasco da Gama, while sailing up the coast of East Africa, wrote of capturing a barca or ocean-going vessel. "In the one we took we found seventeen men, besides gold, silver, an abundance of maize [*milho*] and other provisions."

M. D. W. Jeffreys, in his article "Pre-Columbian Maize in the Old World," believes that these "widespread reports" of maize prior to 1500 "can only be explained by earlier introductions." His article, which he admits is a "linguistic study," cites reports of maize in Castile, Andalusia, Milan, and Portugal, plus extensive cultivation in Morocco and West and East Africa. This evidence, he concludes, "[i]s only compatible with an introduction into Africa about the twelfth century and an introduction into Spain about the thirteenth century." Unfortunately for his theory, he cites no archaeological or ethnobotanical evidence to support the linguistic references. Jeffreys believes that five years is too short a period of time for maize to move from Spain to East Africa and become established there, and he may be right. However, once in Italy it became established quickly in Lombardy and flourishes there to this day, along with rice.

It took longer for maize to be recognized by the herbalists and historians. In 1539, maize is mentioned in the herbal of Hieronymus Bock and in 1543 in the herbal of Leonhard Fuchs. By 1554 maize was extensively cultivated in Polesine de Rovigo and Basso Veronese in Italy, but Waverly Root suggests that it was first grown in the Maccarese region, north of the Tiber River, where it was known as "Roman wheat." In 1556, the historian Gonzalo Fernandez de Oviedo mentioned it being grown near Madrid, but such plantings could have been for animal fodder rather than for human consumption.

Initially, farmers grew maize because it produced more food (and thus more calories) per acre than did other grains. Another reason they grew it was that they could avoid paying taxes on it—the authorities simply did not consider it to be food for humans and did not want to accept it as in-kind taxes or rent. Because of this situation, there were no tax records for maize, and its early spread across Italy and the rest of Europe was not well-tracked. Only after maize attracted the attention of travelers and tax collectors did written records reveal its dispersion.

Maize, in the form of polenta, was exclusively a peasant food and is barely mentioned in the cuisine of the upper class. There is a single reference to it as "coarse wheat" in a soup in Scappi's *Opera*, but in the seventeenth-century cookbooks of Bartolomeo Stefani and Latini, it is called animal fodder.

SCAPPI'S MAIZE SOUP

"Coarse wheat" is a grain much larger than the one used to make bread, and in Lombardy one finds it in quantity. Select it and wash the dirt off of it, and soak it in water for ten hours, changing the water several times. Place it in a pot to cook with fatty meat broth. Add Milanese sausage or a piece of salted pork to give it flavor. Add cinnamon and saffron, cover the pot, and cook it for no less than two and a half hours. Serve with cheese and cinnamon on top. This soup should be very thick and can be enriched with cheese, eggs, and pepper.

Root comments: "Europe resisted this strange new grain except where it borrowed familiarity by resembling foods already known, as in Italy, where it became the chief cereal from which polenta is made, the last in a series dating from Etruscan times." Thus the history of maize in Italy is really the story of the transformation of the ultimate peasant dish, polenta. This porridge or gruel was first made with ground chestnuts, acorns, barley, or wheat. Then millet was the grain of choice (which gave it a golden color), or foxtail (*panico*), which was not cultivated as extensively.

After the introduction of buckwheat around the beginning of the sixteenth century, northern Italians began to use it to make polenta, and the result was a grainy, gray gruel with a sharper flavor. (It is still made this way in the Alpine valleys, where it is known as *polenta taragna*.) After maize was introduced and was widely grown around the middle of the sixteenth century, it was used to make polenta and was accepted not only because it was easy to grow, but because it returned polenta to its familiar golden coloration.

ON POLENTA, I

"As a general rule, the proportion of grain to water is one to two, allowing the absorption and evaporation of the water. A successful batch of polenta requires about forty minutes of close attention, which may account for its scarcity on Italian menus in the United States. When you shop for the makings of polenta, I'd recommend a medium- or coarse-grind, but a trip to an ethnic grocery for a coarser, unlabeled meal is worth the time it takes."

—Lidia Bastianich

But there was a downside to the peasant polenta. Because it was the major part of the diet in the eighteenth and nineteenth centuries, consumed almost exclusively, it resulted in outbreaks of pellagra, a vitamin-deficiency disease caused by a dietary lack of niacin and protein. Symptoms of pellagra are red skin lesions, diarrhea, dermatitis, weakness, mental confusion, and eventually dementia. Corn kernels in the New World that were treated with lime to remove the tough skin of the kernels made niacin available to the body and prevented pellagra, but this technique was not transmitted to Europe. In reality, the polenta did not cause pellagra; the narrow diet of eating only polenta did. Eating a more varied diet would have prevented it, but during lean times, maize was all the commoners had to eat. This was particularly true during the food shortages of the eighteenth century, when peasants had no choice but to grow the most productive food crop available.

ON POLENTA, 2

"In Veneto, polenta is also made with very fine powder which is sometimes white. It is called *polentina bianca*, and being thinner, it is spooned rather than cut. Although equally good, it is not as striking in appearance as the golden mountain that is proudly placed on a board in the middle of the table."

—Anna Del Conte

Polenta is an exremely simple dish that can take on many dimensions. It is a still a tradition, and in the words of Anna Del Conte, author of *Gastronomy of Italy*, "Making it and serving it are a hallowed ritual." The dish is still so popular in Lombardy that Root notes that the "properly equipped family" owns a polenta copper pot, which is a special device used only for the cooking of polenta. And, of course, there must be a favorite stick to stir the basic mixture.

And that's what it is—basic, just cornmeal and salted water. You pour the cornmeal into the boiling water and stir it constantly for an hour or so, and you have polenta. If you thin it out to make a breakfast gruel, that's *polentina*, which is often served with sugar and milk as a breakfast dish. Root notes that the quality of the final dish results from the particular grind of the cornmeal, coarse or fine; whether or not the polenta is removed from the heat or allowed to thicken over it; and the instincts and experience of the individual cook.

ON POLENTA, 3: MAKING IT

"The process is straight forward. You'll need:

> *1 pound or slightly more of coarsely ground corn meal (you want corn meal the consistency of fine to medium-grained sand, not flour, and if possible stone-ground)*
> *2 quarts boiling water (have more handy)*
> *A heaping teaspoon of salt*

Set the water on the fire in a wide bottomed pot and add the salt. When it comes to a boil, add the corn meal in a very slow stream (you don't want the pot to stop boiling), stirring constantly with a wooden spoon to keep lumps from forming. Continue stirring, in the same direction, as the mush thickens, for about a half-hour (the longer you stir the better the polenta will be; the finished polenta should have the consistency of firm mashed potatoes), adding boiling water as necessary.... Making polenta from scratch like this takes a fair amount of effort, because you really do have to stir constantly, or the polenta will stick to the bottom of the pot and burn. If you like polenta, you should consider purchasing a polenta maker, which is a pot with a motor-driven paddle that takes care of the stirring for you."

—Kyle Phillips

When the polenta is thick and creamy, it can be eaten with a little butter and a favorite spice (why not sugar?), or it can turn hard as it dries out. In dry form, polenta is similar to but not as grainy as cornbread but can serve a similar purpose. It can be flavored with pan juices from roasts, tomato sauces, and commercial sauces of all kinds, and the slices can be roasted, toasted, or fried (in butter and olive oil). The slices can then be used as sandwich bread, with fillings of cheese, tomatoes, meat sauce, and sausages, as with *torta di polenta*, or as part of a casserole that could include sausage, mushrooms, and grated cheese.

Other polenta variations include *polenta e ciccioli*, which has pork cracklings and onions added to the polenta near the end of the cooking, making it stiff enough for slicing. It is served, of course, with grated cheese. *Polenta e bagna d'infern* has a very spicy sauce served over it, and the variations go on and on.

The most unusual polenta recipe recounted by Root is *polenta coi osei*, a Venetian specialty that consists of very small songbirds—probably thrushes—that have been wrapped in fat and spit-roasted. Each bird is placed on its own slice of polenta that has been flavored with the drippings from the spit. Root could not resist observing that the birds are caught in wire nets because they are too small to shoot. With polenta, all that changes somehow stays the same, and even the older traditions are still intact. *Paniccio*, the traditional dish of the Feast of St. Anthony the Abbot, is a polenta still made with millet on the day of the feast. In Abruzzo, a large cauldron of millet-based polenta is stirred with wooden paddles, and large chunks of Pecorino cheese are added until the mass turns dark and creamy. Then the polenta is blessed by the priest and the feast begins.

The Second Italian Food Renaissance

After the first food Renaissance, Italian cuisine continued to evolve, and this evolution is recorded in cookbooks like *Archidipno, ovvero dell'insalata e dell'uso di essa* (*Archdipno, or On Salad and Its Uses*), a monumental work published by Salvatore Massonio in 1627. Massonio was a physician who used the Greek word *archidipno* to describe what he considered to be the central part of the meal: a salad composed of greens, flowers, and fruits all mixed together. Twenty years later there was a re-flourishing of classical themes in the work of Giovanni Francesco Vasselli, *L'Apicio overo il maestro de' conviti* (*Apicius, or The Master of Banquets*), proving that Italian cooks were still in awe of Apicius.

In 1662, Bartolomeo Stefani wrote a treatise on Italian regional food entitled *L'arte di ben cucinare* (*The Art of Fine Cooking*), in which he described the "gastronomic districts" like Naples and Sicily that were warm enough in the winter to provide citrus, artichokes, asparagus, and lettuce to other parts of the Italian peninsula. This sort of "food exchange" occurred throughout the not-yet-unified country, with Bologna providing grapes and olives to Lombardy and Florence.

The last great collection of Italian regional recipes was Antonio Latini's *Lo scalco alla moderna* (*The Modern Steward*), published in two volumes from 1692 through 1694. Starting with Naples, he covers the provinces of the peninsula in great detail, describing the regional specialties and giving recipes for their preparation. He concludes: "Naturally, for the sake of brevity, I have listed only the best-known items, since each of the twelve provinces contains as much goodness as you would find in the whole wide world."

The invasion of French cookbooks, both in French and translated into Italian, dominated the Italian culinary scene for nearly a decade after Latini, as exemplified by *Il cuoco piemontese perfezionato a Parigi* (*The Piedmontese Cook Trained in Paris*), which was published in Piedmont in 1766 and reprinted in Venice in 1789 and in Milan in 1791. Somewhat influenced by the French-oriented cookbooks was Vincenzo Corrado's *Il cuoco gallante* (*The Gallant Cook*), published in Naples in 1786, which emphasized local foods prepared with the typical saucing *alla francese*—French-style. However, such recipes were limited to the end of Corrado's book, and again there was a brief resurgence of Italian pride. Still, these were the foods of the nobility, not the dishes served in taverns or the homes of common people. But this was soon to change.

The dichotomy between haute and common cuisine soon led to a new publishing endeavor influenced by domestic notebooks that had recorded the dishes and recipes used by the common folk. *La cucina casereccia* (*Home Cooking*) was first published in Naples in 1807, and it went through twenty-five printings up to 1885; it was also printed in Milan and Palermo. This book was the first real emergence of popular cooking, and it went hand-in-hand with Nicholas Appert's innovative approach to preserving food in Italy in 1810: canning—from a Frenchman!

That year, the Italian translation of Appert's book *L'art de conserver les substances animales et vegetales* (*The Art of Preserving for Several Years All Animal and Vegetable Products*) was published in Siena, and it would forever revolutionize Italian cooking. The food historian Ralph Hancock explains the technique:

Food of any type—meats, soups, fruits, and vegetables—was placed in a stout, wide-mouthed jar, and this was closed with a stopper composed of several layers of cork with the grain running crosswise to reduce porosity. The stopper was sealed with an odd but effective mixture of cheese and lime, and wired down as for champagne. The jars, enclosed in sacking in anticipation of some bursts, were then heated in a water bath. Appert worked out the cooking times for each type of food.

Even though Appert did not understand the scientific reasons for the success of his canning techniques, that fact did not prevent him from capitalizing on it and making it a commercial success all over Europe. A series of manuals, translated from the French beginning in 1824, led to the publication in 1832 of *Manuale del cuoco e del pasticciere* (*Manual for the Cook and Pastry Cook*) by V. Agnoletti. In that book, Agnoletti introduced the new canning method for preserving tomatoes, which would soon become industrialized. "In the case of the tomato," write Alberto Capatti and Massimo Montanari, "which was used above all as a condiment, the new method guaranteed constant availability at a steady cost, summer and winter, without waste. In Italy this would be the preserved food par excellence, spreading to all parts of the country and becoming an aspect of national identity."

In the mid- to late-1800s, Italian cookbooks alternated between those for the professionals and those for housewives. The professionals rejoiced at the publication of *La cucina classica* (*Classical Cuisine*) by Urbain Dubois and Emile Bernard in 1877 (funded by an association of Milanese cooks), which contained, thanks to advances in printing techniques, engravings that showed culinary preparation techniques. On the other side, booklets, like *La cuoca cremonese* (*The Cook of Cremona*), that began publication in the late 1700s and continued for a century or more were inexpensive and included lists of available products, menus, and recipes.

The next great Italian cookbook was Pellegrino Artusi's *La scienza in cucina e l'arte di mangiar bene* (*Science in Cooking and the Art of Good Eating*), which was published in 1891. Although Artusi did not cover every region of Italy, ignoring the south except for Sicily, his book became a symbol of Italian cuisine. He journeyed all around Italy, recording his culinary experiences and collecting recipes, and his style was to explain everything. He was authoritative but not pedantic, and besides the memoirs and recipes, he was firmly grounded in kitchen science.

Artusi also led the way to standardizing the Italian used in cookbooks, removing much of the French terminology and leading to Alfredo Pan-zini's *Dizionario moderno* (*Modern Dictionary*) in 1905, which promoted *italianita*, or Italianess. Beginning on January 1, 1908, the menus in the remaining royal courts were written entirely in Italian, not French, and the following year, Alberto Cougnet, author of the authoritative *L'arte cucinaria in Italia* (*Culinary Art in Italy*) praised Artusi as "the inspirer of this perceptible national reform to achieve a terminology and a language that is properly Italian." Also in 1910 came the publication of V. Agnetti's *Cucina nazionale* (*National Cooking*). The curse of the French influence on Italian cuisine was finally lifted.

After World War I, with Italian immigrants flooding into the United States, it was only natural that Italian cookbooks in English would follow. In 1919, the Italian Cook Book Company in New York published *The Italian Cook Book: The Art Of Eating Well, Practical Recipes Of The Italian Cuisine, Pastries, Sweets, Frozen Delicacies, And Syrups*, compiled by Maria Gentile. The preface to the book states:

> In the Italian cuisine we find in the highest degree these three qualities. That it is palatable, all those who have partaken of food in an Italian trattoria or at the home of an Italian fam-ily can testify, that it is healthy the splendid manhood and womanhood of Italy is a proof more than sufficient. And who could deny, knowing the thriftiness of the Italian race, that it is economical?

This particular cookbook was one of seventy-five chosen for Michigan State University's Feeding America: The Historic American Cookbook Project, which selected classic cookbooks dating from 1798 to 1922. The project calls *The Italian Cook Book* one of the more influential American cookbooks ever published. Jan Longone, curator of American culinary history at the University of Michigan's Clements Library, comments: "If we can get by the stereotyping, we find an early variety of the modern Mediterranean Diet syndrome!"

Back in Italy, in 1935 Lidia Morelli's *Nuovo ricettario domestico* (*New Domestic Recipe Collection*) was published, and it offered 5,390 entries on everyday life, including, in addition to recipes and instructions on how to compile them, essays on hygiene and health. Fifteen years later in 1950, Italy's bestselling culinary "bible," *Il Cucchino d'argentino* (*The Silver Spoon*), was published, with more than 2,000 recipes. After selling more than one million copies in many editions in Italy, in 2005, it was translated into English and published by Phaidon Press in a 1,264-page volume entitled *The Silver Spoon*.

FROM THE FIRST U.S. ITALIAN COOKBOOK, PART I

Polenta con Salsicce
(*Corn Meal with Sausages*)

Cook in water one cup of yellow cornmeal making a stiff mush. Salt it well and when it is cooked spread out to cool on a bread board about half an inch thick. Then cut the mush into small squares. Put in a saucepan several whole sausages with a little water, and when they are cooked skin and crush them and add some brown stock or tomato sauce. Put the polenta (or cornmeal mush) in a fireproof receptacle, season with grated cheese, the crushed sausages and a piece of butter. Put it in the oven and serve when hot.

—from *The Italian Cook Book: The Art Of Eating Well, Practical Recipes Of The Italian Cuisine, Pastries, Sweets, Frozen Delicacies, And Syrup*, 1919

The American interest in Italian food was piqued by two books by expatriate food historian Waverly Root. In 1968, Time Life Books published *The Cooking of Italy* as part of its Foods of the World series. The project was actually two books, a large-format hardcover with many color photos and a smaller, spiral-bound recipe book to accompany it. Marketed through direct mail solicitations, Root's book and the others in the series were enormously popular during the late sixties and early seventies. Three years later in 1971, Atheneum published Root's voluminous and authoritative *The Food of Italy*, which proved how much the author knew about Italian food from all of his travels throughout the country. Through Vintage, the book is still in print thirty-five years later, and although it lacks recipes, it is one of the best books ever written on the subject of Italian food and cooking.

FROM THE FIRST U.S. ITALIAN COOKBOOK,
PART 2

Salsa di Pomidoro
(*Tomato Sauce*)

Chop together, fine, one quarter of an onion, a clove of garlic, a piece of celery as long as your finger, a few bay leaves and just enough parsley. Season with a little oil, salt and pepper, cut up seven or eight tomatoes and put everything over the fire together. Stir it from time to time and when you see the juice condensing into a thin custard strain through a sieve, and it is ready for use. When fresh tomatoes are not available the tomato paste may be used. This is a concentrated paste made from tomatoes and spices which is to be had at all Italian grocers, now so numerous in all American cities. Thinned with water, it is a much used ingredient in Italian recipes. Catsup and concentrated tomato soup do not make satisfactory substitutes as they are too sweet in flavor. Of course canned tomatoes seasoned with salt and a bit of bay leaf can always be used instead of fresh tomatoes. This sauce serves many purposes. It is good on boiled meat; excellent to dress macaroni, spaghetti or other pastas which have been seasoned with butter and cheese, or on boiled rice seasoned in the same way (see Risotto). Mushrooms are a fine addition to it.

—from *The Italian Cook Book: The Art Of Eating Well, Practical Recipes Of The Italian Cuisine, Pastries, Sweets, Frozen Delicacies, And Syrup*, 1919

The books by Root launched an explosion of publishing books on Italian cooking which persists to this day. Le Cordon Bleu's *The Book of Cookbooks* (1994) lists eighty-two Italian cookbooks, and most of the titles are in English and German. In February 2006, a search for "Italian cooking" on Amazon.com returned 987 results, more than "French cooking," which returned 911 results.

In the United States, the popularity of Italian-style food is astounding, with thousands of casual-dining chain restaurant units leading the way. The larger chains are The Olive Garden (about 660 restaurants), Romano's Macaroni Grill (about 210 restaurants), and Carrabba's Italian Grill (about 200 restaurants), and there are dozens of smaller Italian chains like Buca di Beppo (about 100 restaurants), Spaghetti Warehouse (about 22 restaurants) and, of course, thousands of independent Italian restaurants. And these figures do not include chain and independent pizzerias, which are deemed to be a separate restaurant category. Regardless of how "authentic" the Italian-style chain restaurants are, they are proof of the enormous popularity of what is perceived to be Italian cuisine.

One of the main reasons for the popularity of its own food in Italy is that the multifaceted cuisine of the country itself has not been overwhelmed by mass-marketed fast food. Alberto Capatti and Massimo Montanari observe:

> Instead of translating itself into the large-scale adoption of ready-to-eat foods, often prepared hundreds of miles from the place of purchase, as occurred in England, Germany, and the United States, Italy's increased wealth has led to the new prestige enjoyed by traditional recipes and products, to a preference for small-scale food producers (which enables their survival), and to the cult status of wine and gastronomy. Home cooking has remained an important criterion in culinary matters, whereas the fast-food business supplies meals to less than 3 percent of the population.

With all due respect to these authors, it should be pointed out that there are about 300 McDonald's units in Italy, and the company claims to serve 600,000 Italians each day, which is about 2,000 people per unit per day.

Even if that is an exaggeration, Italy has been invaded by American fast food; however, it seems to be fighting back. The Slow Food movement, which was founded in Italy in 1986, now has more than 83,000 members around the world, and about half of those are Italians.

SOPHIA AND SPAGHETTI

The great Italian beauty Sophia Loren once famously said, "All you see I owe to spaghetti." But she also had advice on how to eat it. Posted in Italy's Spaghetti Historical Museum in Pontedassio, near Genoa, is her advice on pasta etiquette, "Spaghetti can be eaten successfully if you inhale it like a vacuum cleaner."

Another factor in the popularity of Italian cuisine is the phenomenon known as "The Mediterranean Diet." The discovery of isolated areas where poverty and good health existed together was made in 1945 by an American doctor named Ancel Keys, who was stationed in Salerno, Italy.

Children eating macaroni in the streets of Naples, 1873
North Wind Picture Archives

His Seven Countries Study involved 12,763 men aged forty through fifty-nine. Results showed that men who followed a "Mediterranean diet" had less coronary heart disease. Ancel and Margaret Keys later published their findings in *How to Eat Well and Stay Well the Mediterranean Way* (Double-day, 1959), which was the origin of "The Mediterranean Diet." The Keys presented Italian cooking as a way to combat cholesterol, heart problems, and obesity, mostly through the substitution of olive oil for butter. Capatti and Montanari comment that "[s]un, spaghetti, pizza, and vegetables have now become part of the myth of good health," but many people believe that the Mediterranean diet works.

The common Mediterranean dietary pattern has these characteristics:

- High consumption of fruits, vegetables, bread and other cereals, potatoes, beans, nuts, and seeds
- Olive oil is an important monounsaturated fat source
- Dairy products, fish, and poultry are consumed in low to moderate amounts, and little red meat is eaten
- Eggs are consumed zero to four times a week
- Wine is consumed in low to moderate amounts

The Mediterranean Diet Cookbook by Nancy Harmon Jenkins was published by Bantam Books in 1994, and it led to a plethora of books on the subject. A search of Amazon.com in March 2006 for "Mediterranean diet" returned 153 results. There are numerous variations on the theme in this mini-industry, including *Olive Oil Cookery: The Mediterranean Diet*; *My New Mediterranean Cookbook: Eat Better, Live Longer by Following the Mediterranean Diet*; *The Mediterranean Diet: Wine, Pasta, Olive Oil, and a Long, Healthy Life*; and *The Mediterranean Heart Diet: How It Works and How to Reap the Health Benefits, with Recipes to Get You Started*.

As we have seen in chapter five, Leonardo himself followed most of the precepts of the Mediterranean diet, as he ate little or no red meat, while consuming lots of vegetables and a moderate amount of wine.

Feste! The Food Festivals

Whether it's a *feria* (holiday), a *fiera* (trade show), *festa* (festival), or *sagra* (religion-based festival), you can be sure that there will be plenty of food at a celebration in Italy. In a twist upon Renaissance festivals, where the commoners were often invited to watch the courtiers at feast—but not indulge—the Italian food festivals of today include everyone. "Festivals are still part of the dance of life, the great feast at the moment of plenty," writes Carol Field, author of *Celebrating Italy*. "They are moments when people can have their culture and eat it too."

Regardless of whether the foods have ancient traditions or were more recently introduced, the Italians have adopted the "any excuse for a party" attitude about them. Take polenta, for example. Who would think that such a basic food, with a thousand-year tradition but now almost exclusively based on maize (which the rest of Europe regards as animal fodder), could inspire such frenzies of consumption? There are numerous celebrations of polenta, from a simple dinner of *polenta taragna*, buckwheat polenta layered with gorgonzola cheese, for the Eve of Epiphany (January 5) to the huge *Polentonissimo* in Piedmont or the *Polentata* in Emilia-Romagna that feeds an entire village several times over.

The *Polentonissimo* is celebrated each March 6 at the monastery of Bormida and recalls the generosity of the Marchese Rovere, who saved some coppersmiths from starving during a snowstorm by feeding them polenta and a frittata. These days the feast is based on a huge amount of polenta that is covered with a sauce of sausage and salami, plus an eighty-five-pound onion frittata. Both dishes are served in the town piazza to the delight of nearby residents and visitors from all over.

On the last Tuesday of Carnival, the small village of Tossignano sets up copper cauldrons in the center of their piazza for the cooking of about 500 pounds of cornmeal. The cooks, dressed appropriately in yellow jackets, stir the polenta continuously in the same direction with wooden paddles. A band plays while the cooks pour the polenta onto a gigantic table and then cut it into slices. The slices are placed into a metal-lined container along with more than 300 pounds of sausage, ground beef, and pancetta, plus nearly sixty pounds of Parmesan cheese that comprises the *polenta pasticciata*, which is then served to everyone attending the festival. Interestingly, a rival festival devoted to pasta is held on the same day in nearby Borgo Tossignano, with more than two tons of pasta being served, also containing sausages, beef, and Parmesan cheese. So take your choice, maize or durum wheat!

It is not surprising that pasta, Italy's favorite food, is served in all its forms at many of the festivals, but it's not on the menu at the *Festa del Riso* in Villimpenta on the last Sunday in May. We would expect that some version of risotto would be served, but instead *riso alla pilota* is the main dish, a sort of pilaf that besides Arborio rice contains pork tenderloin, pancetta in a sausage that's called *pesto*, and lots of Parmesan cheese. It is named after the huskers, the *pilotata*, who removed the outer skin of the grains of rice in the old days.

The small festival celebrates the time of rice planting and features large copper cauldrons atop roaring wood fires, and the rice is cooked in spring water all at once. When most of the water has evaporated, the fire is put out, the cauldron is covered with blankets, and the rice steams until completely done. Then the cooks mix in the *pesto* sausage, and the *riso alla pilota* is served accompanied with bread from nearby Ferrara. Another signature rice dish, *risi e bisi* (rice and peas), is served on April 25 in Venice and environs, as part of the Feast Day of San Marco, the patron saint.

PASTA PROVERBS

"No man is lonely while eating spaghetti."

—Robert Morley

"Marriage is not merely the sharing of the fettuccine, but sharing the burden of finding the fettuccine restaurant in the first place."

—Calvin Trillin

"Give us this day our daily taste. Give us pasta with a hundred fillings."

—Robert Farrar Capon

"Pasta and macaroni, the hotter the better."

—Corsican saying

"If you ate pasta and antipasta, would you still be hungry?"

—attributed to comedian Steven Wright

Since wine is such an important part of Italian cuisine, it is only natural that there should be numerous *feste* devoted to grapes and their main reason for existence. In September and October, across most of Italy a festival devoted to wine called *La Sagra dell'Uva* is held. The most famous location for this celebration is Marino, near Rome. Herbert Kubly, author of *An American in Italy*, described the *Fiera dell'Uva* in Marino as "sort of a wedding of the Virgin Mary with the grape god Bacchus followed by a *bacchanalia* at which the fountains flowed with wine instead of water." The first festival in Marino occurred in 1571 to honor the victory of Christian forces over the Turks at the Battle of Lepanto, and they've been partying ever since.

A different sort of wine *festa* is held at Greve in Chianti. Instead of *bacchanalia*, it's more business at a trade fair that's devoted to the wines of the Chianti Classico district. The elaborate wine tasting goes on for five days and nights accompanied by concerts, dances, and sporting events, but no massive feasts. Some nights the residents dress up in medieval and Renaissance costumes, and, accompanied by drummers and trumpeters, they are wildly greeted as they flood into the piazza. As can be imagined, the cafés, butcher shops, and bakeries are flooded with hungry visitors and residents seeking something to eat while they taste the wines.

There are too many wine festivals to cover in great detail, but a few of the others can be briefly mentioned. The *Sagra dell'Uva* at Quartu Sant'Elena in Sardinia features not only grapes and wines but sweets based on the almonds that grow everywhere. At the *Sagra dell'Uva* held in Merano, near the Austrian border, wine competes with beer for the attention of the revelers; the signs are all in German, and since the event is held in October, the usual comparisons to Oktoberfest are made. And during the *Vendemmia*, the crushing of the grapes in Alba and Todi in Piedmont, it is traditional to serve *bagna cauda*, that hot bath of olive oil, anchovies, and garlic that is used as a dip for fall vegetables such as red bell peppers, celery, and leeks.

SLIM PICKINGS

In 1957, the BBC broadcasted a short film titled *Spaghetti Picking in the Spring*, which supposedly showed life in the countryside outside of Lugano. A very serious announcer described a tree which produced dozens of pounds of spaghetti, and he went on to explain that thanks to knowledge acquired over generations, the trees produced spaghetti of equal length, which assisted the spaghetti pickers. The following day, the BBC studios were inundated with phone calls from people who were interested in buying the spaghetti trees and wanted the phone numbers of retailers.

Sweets, or *dolci*, are the legacy of the fanatical Italian love of sugar that began in the early Renaissance and is evident today in the astounding variety of sugary goodies from all regions. Besides all the various incarnations of sugar, there is the twenty-one-foot-high, one-ton-plus Cake of the Fieschi in Lavagna near Genoa. It is created for the August 14 celebration that honors the marriage of Count·Opizzo Fieschi, the lord of Lavagna, to Bianca de Bianchi in 1230. The wedding is reenacted amidst fencing contests, dances in period costumes, a candlelight parade of knights and squires, and much fantasy merriment as guys with fake name tags (like Francesco) must meet up with their female counterparts (Francesca) in order to sample slices of the pyramid-shaped cake in the piazza. Sad to say, it is not the largest cake in the world; that honor goes to a cake in Las Vegas, Nevada, that in 2005 measured 102 feet long, 52 feet wide, and a mere 20 inches high, but it weighed 26 tons, which is considerably more than the 2 tons of the Lavagna cake. How about Lavagna having the *tallest* cake in the world? We'll see. The entire cake is consumed in a mere two hours!

It is natural and traditional that sweet delicacies such as *spongata*, the honeyed nut cake from Parma, should be served at Christmas, and that various sugary breads should be prepared for Easter, but what does one serve when celebrating the return of the dead? Bones, of course. We have already seen sugar bones created for various Renaissance feasts, and the tradition lives on in the form of *osso da morto*, "bones of the dead," that are eaten during All Souls' Day. Referred to in Italy as *Il Morto*, "the Dead," the holiday is the period between the first and second nights in November. These bones are composed of egg whites, finely chopped almonds, and sugar, which are formed into skeletons. They are accompanied by *fave dei morte*, little cookies shaped like fava beans, which are symbolic of the dead since Roman times because they supposedly contain their souls. But this celebration is neither sad nor morbid, for the children write notes to their departed relatives, who return on All Souls' Day and bring the bones to their descendants as a treat.

Another kind of sweet is featured during an eight-day festival in Perugia—chocolate. Eurochocolate, held in October, may be the largest food *festa* in the country, with organizers claiming one million attendees for the event. There are a total of 700 booths, with 130 of them featuring small, artisan producers of chocolate treats. Celebrating what Italians believe is the "food of the gods," the unique combination of festival and fair has exhibitions, laboratories, cooking classes, tastings, celebrations, and a "C8" summit of the world's eight largest cocoa-manufacturing countries. Best of all, the streets are filled with booths selling anything and everything related to chocolate.

SWEET MACARONI

Here is a classic chocolate dessert recipe from Perugia, home of the Eurochocolate festival.

Prepare the pasta in the usual way using water and flour but not eggs. Boil and drain it, then season it with chocolate powder, sugar, cinnamon, chopped walnuts, and grated lemon rind. You can use as much of each ingredient as you like, to taste. Mix well and serve cold.

Most of the vendors are located in the streets of Perugia's historical center, but booths can also be found underground, in the magnificent Rocca Paolina—renamed "Rocca Pralina" during Eurochocolate. It's a stronghold built by Pope Paul III in 1540, and later the Perugians simply built their city on top of it.

Every year, the organizers come up with a theme, like *Ottobre Rosso* (Red October) in 2005, when they featured a "new" chocolate flavor trend: hot chile peppers. And there's reason to believe this flavor will stay popular for quite a while—after all, combining chocolate and chiles dates back to the Maya in Central America thousands of years ago.

Some of the Eurochocolate highlights, sponsored by a large Perugia chocolate manufacturer, are the sculptures created by artists from giant solid blocks of chocolate, with the public watching and enjoying the chips and chunks they carve off.

Several festivals celebrate those late-adopted fruits that have now become so popular in Italy, tomatoes and chile peppers, or *peperoncini*. Sardinia has two festivals for tomatoes, one in Cagliari in July and the other in Oristano in August, while Sicily's fest is in Ragusa in May. The tomato processing town of Angri, between Salerno and Naples, has its festival in September. But these small festivals pale in comparison to the Peperoncino Festival, which is held to honor the tomato's close relative.

Since Columbus was responsible for the introduction of chile peppers into Europe, it was only fitting that the first Peperoncino Festival was held in 1992, 500 years after he found them in the New World. Organized by the *Accademia Italiana del Peperoncino*, or the Italian Pepper Academy, and its leader, Enzo Monaco, the festival started out small but in recent years has drawn many thousands of visitors to the small town of Diamante in Calabria, the "toe" of the "boot" that is Italy. The festival is held for four days surrounding the first weekend in September on the *Lungomare*, the promenade on Diamante's seaside. The Italian and other European "chileheads" are drawn by a unique blend of a chile vendor market, music, movies, satire, art, folklore, and samplings from local restaurants. More than 100 vendors have booths offering up everything imaginable related to the beloved *peperoncini*, including:

- *Salsiccia*, a lean pork sausage with fennel seed and peperoncini
- *La bomba*, a sort of spiced-up sangria
- A Calabrian *peperoncino* chocolate liquor called *crema di cacao al peperoncino*

- Pungent *peperoncino* pasta products
- *Grappa al peperoncino di calabria*, the famous Italian grape brandy in a kicked-up version with chiles floating in the bottle
- *Olio santo* (holy oil), bright red chile-infused olive oil in decorative bottles
- *Alici al peperoncino*, a Calabrian specialty, freshly hatched sardines densely packed with *peperoncini* and some salt
- A plethora of sweet heat products, including *baci di Casanova*, dark chocolates with a creamy-smooth chile-spiced center; *confettura di peperoncino al cioccolato*, a spicy chile-chocolate spread; *crostata piccante*, a short pastry tart with a spicy-sweet icing; *cannoli al peperoncino*, crunchy pastry pipes filled with vanilla creme, spiced up with plenty of peperoncini bits; and *dolce della nonna al peperoncino*, Grandma's sponge cake with a kick
- *Vinagra*, a red wine infused with chiles

As evidenced by the Peperoncino Festival, the New World foods continue to make a major impact in Italy today, with peppers now following a path similar to that of tomatoes and corn.

And how the concept of feasting has changed over the centuries! From grand royal feasts that merely allowed the common people to witness the spectacle, now the common people do the feasting in public during festivals that focus on favorite foods. In private situations, everyone eats together with no separation by rank or gender. "Class snobbery and social division are all still firmly in place but tempered by the possibility of Everyman gaining admittance," adds Roy Strong.

And the star of Italian cuisine, which has been rising over the past five centuries, still shines brightly.

Salsiccia con Polenta
(Sausage with Polenta)

The Italians are very creative when it comes to serving polenta. They sometimes use it to make a kind of lasagne, or serve a wide variety of sauces over it,
including this one. Feel free to substitute other meats for the sausage.

INGREDIENTS

2 slices pancetta or bacon
½ rib celery, chopped
2 cloves garlic
3 tablespoons olive oil
1 onion, chopped
3 Italian sausages, coarsely chopped
2 bay leaves
2 teaspoons tomato paste
½ cup dry white wine
1 cup canned crushed tomatoes
1 cup chicken stock
2 tablespoons Italian parsley, minced
1 basic recipe for polenta, kept warm (see "On Polenta, 3: Making
  It," p. 175)
Salt and freshly ground pepper, to taste

Combine the pancetta, celery, and garlic in a food processor and puree to
a fine paste. In a pot, heat the olive oil and sauté the onion until soft, about 2
minutes. Add the sausage and the processed paste and cook for 5 minutes over
medium heat. Add the bay leaves, tomato paste, and wine and cook for another
5 minutes. Add the tomatoes, the chicken stock, and salt and pepper to taste,
reduce the heat, and simmer for 30 minutes.

Serve the sauce over warm slices of polenta.

YIELD: 4 servings

Peperonata

This recipe originated in southern Italy, where peppers first entered Italian cuisine. In appreciation of the fact that *peperoncini* are now beloved in the region, a fresh red chile pepper has been added to spice it up.

INGREDIENTS

¼ cup olive oil
2 medium onions, peeled and thinly sliced
1 clove garlic, thinly sliced
4 red or yellow bell peppers, seeds and stems removed, thinly sliced
    into vertical strips
1 red jalapeño chile, seeds and stem removed, finely chopped
1 pound plum tomatoes, peeled and chopped
1 tablespoon Italian parsley, minced
Freshly ground black pepper, to taste

Heat the olive oil in a large skillet and add the onion. Sauté over medium heat until the onion is soft, then add the garlic, bell peppers, and jalapeño and cook for about 10 minutes, stirring often.

Add the tomatoes, reduce the heat, and simmer for about 30 minutes, stirring occasionally. Add the parsley and pepper just before serving and stir well.

YIELD: 4 servings

Penne all'Arrabiata
(Enraged Pasta)

Of all the spicy Calabrian dishes served at the Peperoncino Festival, this one is probably the best known. Feel free to increase the heat scale by adding more peperoncini.

INGREDIENTS

2 tablespoons olive oil
2 to 3 medium onions, chopped
2 to 3 cloves garlic, finely chopped
2 small fresh chile pods, red, hot (Thai, serrano, or birdseye),
    seeds and stems removed, finely chopped
2 14-ounce cans chopped tomatoes
1 pound penne rigate pasta
3½ ounces grated Parmesan cheese
Pinch of sugar and salt

In a pan, heat the olive oil over low heat. Add the onions, garlic, and chile and cook until the onions are golden brown. Add the tomatoes and cook, uncovered, for about 15 minutes over low to medium heat.

Meanwhile cook the pasta *al dente* in lightly salted water, according to the instructions on the package.

Grate the Parmesan cheese and stir half of it into the sauce. Season with salt and sugar to taste.

Drain the pasta well, mix thoroughly with the sauce, and sprinkle with the remaining Parmesan cheese. Serve piping hot.

YIELD: 4 servings

Torta di Ricotta
(Italian Cheesecake)

Here's a classic dessert served at Renaissance-era court feasts and at festivals today. As with so many Renaissance dishes, this cake is heavily seasoned. Use the extra egg white from the pastry in the filling.

INGREDIENTS

FOR THE PASTRY:
1 cup flour
4 tablespoons butter at room temperature
1 egg yolk
A little cold water

FOR THE FILLING:
1 pound ricotta cheese
2 eggs
1 egg white
3 tablespoons sugar
1½ teaspoons powdered ginger
½ teaspoon ground cinnamon
2 tablespoons raisins

Preheat the oven to 350° F.

To make the pastry, mix the flour, butter, and egg yolk together in a bowl and add cold water until the dough consistency is right. Knead the dough a little bit and then roll it out on a floured board. Place the dough in a 9-inch pie pan.

To make the filling, combine all ingredients except the raisins in a blender and puree until smooth. Fold in the raisins and pour the filling into the dough. Smooth the top and bake for 40 minutes.

YIELD: 6 servings

Almond Polenta Cake

Although technically not true polenta, the New World cornmeal here is combined with Arab-introduced lemons and the favorite nut of the Renaissance, almonds.

INGREDIENTS

FOR THE CAKE:
8 ounces butter, softened
2 lemon rinds, finely grated
1 cup caster sugar
3 eggs, separated
¼ cup lemon juice
1½ cups ground almonds
1 cup fine polenta (cornmeal)

FOR THE SYRUP:
¼ cup lemon juice
¼ cup sugar

Preheat the oven to 350° F. Lightly grease and flour a 9-inch round cake pan.

In a bowl, beat the butter, rind, and sugar, until light and fluffy. Slowly add the egg yolks, beating well. Stir in the juice, ground almonds, and polenta.

Whip the egg whites until soft peaks form. Carefully fold into the batter mixture.

Spoon the mixture into the prepared pan. Bake for about 50 minutes or until a toothpick inserted in the center comes out clean.

To make the syrup, boil the lemon juice and sugar in a small saucepan, stirring until the sugar is dissolved. Spoon the syrup over the hot cake wedges.

YIELD: 6 servings

FURTHER READING

Below, by subject, are the most significant references that I consulted for this book. A complete bibliography for the entire project of *Da Vinci's Kitchen*, including the printed edition and the online-only material, is available at: www.davinciskitchen.com.

A NOTE ON THE NOTEBOOKS

The totality of the thousands of pages of Leonardo's codices has not been translated and is not available to the general public. For the purposes of this book, I have used the two-volume Dover edition of the selected works of Leonardo first published as *The Literary Works of Leonardo da Vinci* in 1883 by Jean Paul Richter and now titled *The Notebooks of Leonardo da Vinci*. I also consulted *The Notebooks of Leonardo da Vinci*, selected and edited by Irma A. Richter, the daughter of Jean Paul Richter (Oxford University Press, 1952). For a complete listing of all the codices, their physical location, and their content, consult *Leonardo: The Universal Man* by Alessandra Fregolent.

LEONARDO DA VINCI

Bramly, Serge. *Leonardo: The Artist and the Man*. New York: Penguin Books, 1994.

Clark, Kenneth. *Leonardo da Vinci*. London: Penguin Books, 1993.

Da Vinci, Leonardo. *The Notebooks of Leonardo da Vinci*. Ed. Irma A. Richter. Oxford: Oxford University Press, 1998.

Da Vinci, Leonardo. *The Notebooks of Leonardo da Vinci*. Ed. Jean Paul Richter. New York: Dover Publications, 1970.

Fregolent, Alessandra. *Leonardo: The Universal Man*. San Diego: Thunder Bay Press, 2004.

Hurwitz, David. "Leonardo da Vinci's Ethical Vegetarianism." *History of Vegetarianism*. 19 July 2002. www.ivu.org/history/davinci/hurwitz.html.

Nicholl, Charles. *Leonardo da Vinci: Flights of the Mind*. New York: Viking, 2004.

Reti, Ladislao, ed. *The Unknown Leonardo*. New York: McGraw-Hill, 1974.

Spencer, Colin. *The Heretic's Feast: A History of Vegetarianism*. Hanover, NH: University Press of New England, 1995.

Turner, A. Richard. *Inventing Leonardo*. New York: Alfred A. Knopf, 1993.

Vasari, Georgio. *Lives of the Artists, Volume I*. New York: Penguin Books, 1965.

Vezzosi, Alessandro. *Leonardo da Vinci: The Mind of the Renaissance*. New York: Harry N. Abrams, 1996.

White, Michael. *Leonardo: The First Scientist*. New York: St. Martin's Press, 2000.

Zöllner, Frank. *Leonardo da Vinci: The Complete Paintings and Drawings*. Köln, Germany: Taschen, 2000.

Foodstuffs

Davidson, Alan, ed. *The Oxford Companion to Food*. New York: Oxford University Press, 1999.

Flandrin, Jean-Louis, Massimo Montanari, and Albert Sonnenfeld. *Food: A Culinary History*. New York: Columbia University Press, 1999.

Mintz, Sidney W. *Sweetness and Power: The Place of Sugar in Modern History*. New York: Viking Penguin, 1985.

Root, Waverly. *Food: An Authoritative and Visual History and Dictionary of the Foods of the World*. New York: Simon & Schuster, 1980.

Serventi, Silvano, and Francoise Sabban. *Pasta: The Story of a Universal Food*. New York: Columbia University Press, 2002.

Tannahill, Reay. *Food in History*. New York: Crown Publishers, 1973.

Toussaint-Samat, Maguelonne. *History of Food*. Cambridge, MA: Blackwell Reference, 1992.

Trager, James. *The Food Chronology: A Food Lover's Compendium of Events and Anecdotes, from Prehistory to the Present*. New York: Henry Holt, 1995.

Wright, Clifford A. *A Mediterranean Feast: The Story of the Birth of the Celebrated Cuisines of the Mediterranean from the Merchants of Venice to the Barbary Corsairs, with More than 500 Recipes*. New York: William Morrow & Co., 1999.

RENAISSANCE FOOD

Delle Cinqueterre, Berengario. *The Renaissance Cookbook*. Crown Point, IA: Dunes Press, 1975.

Martino, Maestro. *Libro de arte coquinaria*. Rome c. 1465. The Katherine Bitting Collection, Library of Congress. CD-ROM. Oakland, CA: Octavo, 2003.

Redon, Odile, Francoise Sabban, and Silvano Serventi. *The Medieval Kitchen: Recipes from France and Italy*. Chicago: University of Chicago Press, 1998.

Riley, Gillian. "Renaissance in the Kitchen." *Libro de arte coquinaria*. By Maestro Martino. Rome c. 1465. The Katherine Bitting Collection, Library of Congress. CD-ROM. Oakland, CA: Octavo, 2003.

———. *Renaissance Recipes*. San Francisco: Pomegranate Artbooks, 1993.

Sacchi, Bartolomeo (Platina). *Platina: On Right Pleasure and Good Health*. Ed. Mary Ella Milham. Tempe, AZ: Medieval & Renaissance Texts & Studies, 1998.

Santich, Barbara. *The Original Mediterranean Cuisine: Medieval Recipes for Today*. Chicago: Chicago Review Press, 1995.

Scappi, Bartolomeo. *Opera dell'arte del cucinare*. Testi Antichi di Gastronomia 12. Ed. Giancarlo Roversi. Arnoldo Forni Editore, 1981.

Strong, Roy. *Feast: A History of Grand Eating*. New York: Harcourt, 2002.

ITALIAN CUISINE

Capatti, Alberto, and Massimo Montanari. *Italian Cuisine: A Cultural History*. New York: Columbia University Press, 2003.

Del Conte, Anna. *Gastronomy of Italy*. New York: Prentice Hall Press, 1987.

Evans, Matthew, Gabriella Cossi, and Peter D'Onghia. *World Food: Italy*. Oakland, CA: Lonely Planet Publications, 2000.

Famularo, Joe. *A Cook's Tour of Italy*. New York: HP Books, 2003.

Field, Carol. *Celebrating Italy: The Tastes and Traditions of Italy as Revealed Through Its Feasts, Festivals, and Sumptuous Foods*. New York: William Morrow & Co., 1990.

Gentile, Maria. *The Italian Cook Book: The Art Of Eating Well, Practical Recipes Of The Italian Cuisine, Pastries, Sweets, Frozen Delicacies, And Syrups*. New York: Italian Cook Book Company, 1919.

Roden, Claudia. *Claudia Roden's The Food of Italy: Region by Region*. South Royalton, VT: Steerforth Press, 2003.

Root, Waverly. *The Cooking of Italy*. New York: Time Life Books, 1968.
————. *The Food of Italy*. New York: Vintage Books, 1992.
Touring Club of Italy. *The Italian Food Guide: The Ultimate Guide to the Regional Foods of Italy*. Milan: Touring Editore, 2002.

ABOUT THE AUTHOR

Dave DeWitt is a writer, editor, and show producer. He is the author of more than 50 books, mostly on food history, chile peppers, and spicy foods. Not only is he the publisher of the Fiery Foods & Barbecue SuperSite (Fiery-Foods.com), he's the founding producer of the National Fiery Foods & Barbecue Show since 1988. Dave lives with his wife Mary Jane Wilan in the South Valley of Albuquerque with his garden, greenhouse, and an assortment of dogs and cats.

INDEX

NOTE: Page numbers in **bold** indicate an illustration.

Appendix I

Recipes
(Modern Version)

Appendix II

RECIPES

(CLASSIC VERSION)

Printed in Great Britain
by Amazon

14478130R00127